The World:
Your Oyster

2nd edition

A guide to preparing your game for international distribution.

About This Guide

This guide aims to present, as succinctly and accessibly as possible, how to choose markets for publishing a video game, how to engage the local players, and what other factors to keep in mind during development.

This guide should prove to be useful to:
1.   Video game producers, game project managers, and product managers. You will learn how to choose markets for releasing and publishing games, what to consider before entering these markets, and how to plan a game's development while taking its subsequent localization into account, all from the perspective of maximizing your profits in these markets.
2.   Marketing managers from video game companies. This guide will pitch you ideas for marketing campaigns and in-game events that will help you popularize your game and increase the average player check and LTV.
3.   Localization managers and translators. This guide will help you provide a better localization service and enable your clients to achieve success in markets that are new to them.

Authors:

Denis Khamin, CMO and co-founder, Allcorrect Group. Has worked in software and game localization since 2006, periodically writes for GALA, speaker at conferences on localization and culturalization.

Valentin Pronin, editor, Allcorrect. Worked on localization and voice-over for The Crew 2, Trials Rising, Just Dance series, Need for Speed Heat, and other projects for Ubisoft, EA, and Gaijin.

A big thank you to our clients EA, Ubisoft, Daedalic, Youzoo, Bandai Namco, Fatshark, Gaijin, G5, and many more. You inspire us, allow us to make our own mistakes (some of which wound up as culturalization cases in this book), and help fix those.

Special thanks to Kefir! for pushing us to write this guide.

We'd love to hear your suggestions—you can contact us at pr@allcorrectgames.com.

The printed version of this guide comes with a list of hyperlinked sources. To open the reference list, please use the link http://bit.ly/culturalization.

1. How to Choose a Market for Publishing a Game

In 2016, mobile games became the largest segment in terms of revenue size[1] due to organic growth, and the cannibalization of PC and console games' share of the market.

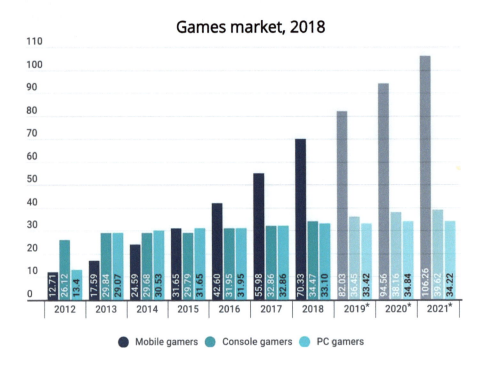

Games market, 2018

During this time, all segments of games that were played from a computer and previously counted separately—including browser-based games, social games, online games with downloadable clients, downloadable casual games, single-player games, and some others—have been combined into a single segment: PC games[2].

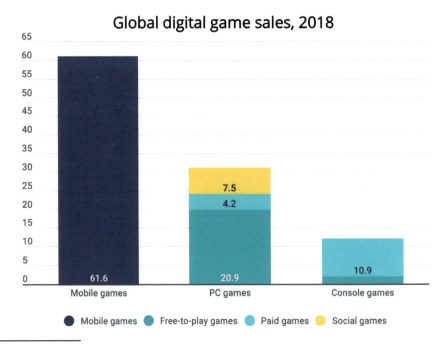

Global digital game sales, 2018

---

[1] PCs to Become the Smallest Gaming Platform in 2018, Newzoo
[2] Digital games industry revenue worldwide in 2018, by game category, Superdata Games with the free-to-play and pay-to-play monetization models have been combined into the so-called nominally free-to-play games segment for the sake of convenience.

Mobile games have grown from small services controlled by mobile operators into a separate video game segment—a primary segment, as a matter of fact.

In this sense, consoles are probably the most conservative segment of them all, but it has also seen changes in the recent past. Indie developers can now add their games to the online platforms of the three primary console manufacturers (Sony, Nintendo, and Microsoft). Indie hits and nominally free-to-play cross-platform online games started to appear alongside with traditional AAA games.

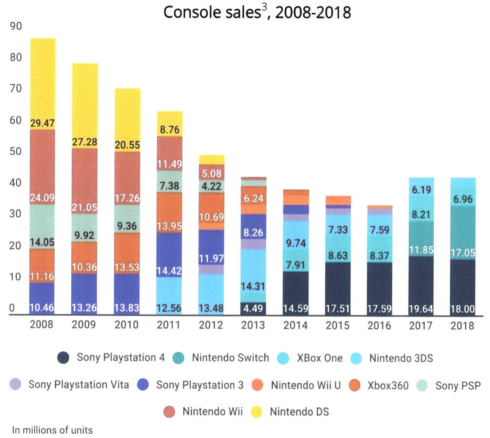

Console sales[3], 2008-2018

In millions of units

The division into three primary segments has become somewhat arbitrary for many games, since they support all platforms in all segments and make money from all types of players. A good example would be Fortnite, which can be played on smartphones, PCs, and all modern consoles, including the Nintendo Switch.

There are currently at least two game engines that make it possible to develop games for all platforms, including mobile: Unity and Unreal. There are also engines that can be used to make commercial games without knowing any programming languages. These include GameMaker Studio (probably the most popular indie engine), Stencyl, Defold, Buildbox, Visionaire Studio, RPG Maker, and others.

---

[3] Global unit sales of current generation video game consoles from 2008 to 2018, VGChartz

In order to publish a game in a particular country, you will be required to (in addition to everything else) have an age rating assigned to your game in accordance with local law. When it comes to releasing a digital copy on most platforms, this process is simplified. If you want to publish a game on physical media, the requirements of local laws, as well as the complexity and cost of getting an age rating, become an additional factor when choosing a market.

When choosing a market in which to publish games you need to consider several factors, including the game's genre, competition, and the market volume. Some market-selection models (such as our ROLI for mobile markets) account for two of these three factors. As for everything else, you'll have to rely on general information, as well as your experience and nose for business.

Over the next few years, the video game markets in Asia, including Southeastern Asia, will slow their growth (in addition, releasing a game in China, Vietnam, and many other Asian countries involves legal and technical challenges), and, due to the growing penetration of Internet and mobile technology, the new drivers of the video game market will be countries in Africa and the Middle East. These markets will grow primarily thanks to mobile games, and any issues with payments and monetization in general, as well as challenges involving localization and culturalization risks associated with Muslim culture, will become pervasive in Africa and the Middle East.

It is also possible that games with a subscription-based monetization model will become more widespread.

1.1. Choosing Markets for Console Games

Despite the fact that the sales of consoles in units have been steadily falling over time[4], the console game market remains quite large and console owners can afford to buy plenty of games.

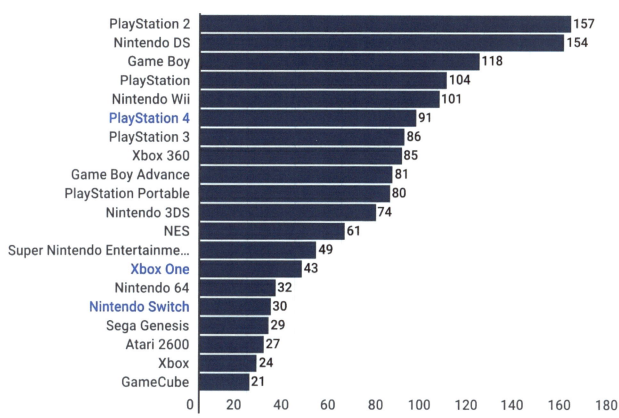

The console market is dominated by two game genres: action adventure games and shooters[5]. There were no indie games whatsoever among the top-selling console games of 2018[6] (unless we count PUBG), and most games were new entries in well-known franchises.

---

[4] Video game console sales worldwide for products total lifespan. VGChartz, February 2019
[5] Top-selling console games worldwide in 2018. VGChartz
[6] Global Yearly Chart. The year's top-selling games at retail ranked by unit sales VGChartz, 2018.

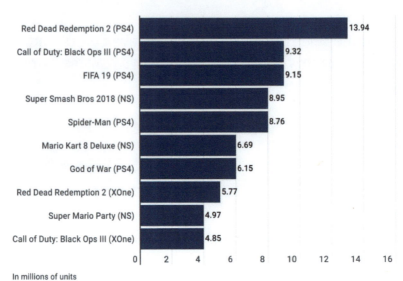

Best-selling console games, 2018

Game	Millions of units
Red Dead Redemption 2 (PS4)	13.94
Call of Duty: Black Ops III (PS4)	9.32
FIFA 19 (PS4)	9.15
Super Smash Bros 2018 (NS)	8.95
Spider-Man (PS4)	8.76
Mario Kart 8 Deluxe (NS)	6.69
God of War (PS4)	6.15
Red Dead Redemption 2 (XOne)	5.77
Super Mario Party (NS)	4.97
Call of Duty: Black Ops III (XOne)	4.85

In millions of units

As far as market share is concerned, Playstation 4 is sitting at the top, while the Nintendo Switch is in third place, but judging by its growth rate, it will become the second most popular console in 2019[7].

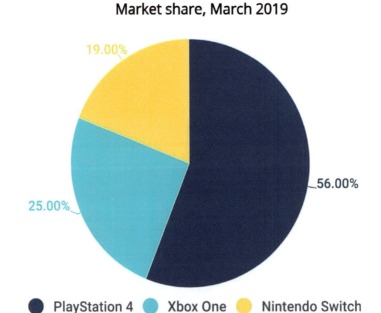

Market share, March 2019

- PlayStation 4 — 56.00%
- Xbox One — 25.00%
- Nintendo Switch — 19.00%

The primary markets for console games will be the USA, Japan, and Western Europe. Keep in mind that every platform has its own requirements when it comes to translating console-related terms. For example, an Xbox controller should be translated into Russian as "геймпад" (gamepad) while a PS controller as "контроллер" (controller). Failing to follow this terminology could lead to your game not being released on a certain platform.

---

[7]PS4 vs. Xbox One vs. Switch: Console and Game Sales Numbers—2019

1.2. Choosing Markets for PC Games

As a rule, PCs are a popular gaming platform in countries where Internet access became widespread before smartphones, and players can't afford consoles or games to play on them.

According to a report from GlobalWebIndex[8], the ten markets where the PC is the most popular gaming platform are:

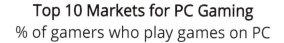

Top 10 Markets for PC Gaming
% of gamers who play games on PC

Egypt	69%
Philippines	65%
Russia	63%
India	60%
Indonesia	55%
Vietnam	54%
Turkey	50%
Taiwan	49%
South Africa	49%
Poland	49%

However, the popularity of PCs absolutely doesn't imply that the PC games segment brings in the most money—in the majority of these countries, the mobile games segment is actually more lucrative.

You should try to determine ahead of time whether you'll be publishing games on physical media or restricting yourself to releasing digital copies in online stores. In the first case, you'll need to undergo the required procedure for getting an age rating for your game in the countries in question, but in the second, the process will be simpler.

It's also important to draw a line between online games that people play on PC and physical or downloadable single-player games.

Primary online PC game stores:
- Steam
- Epic Games Store

---

[8] Gaming: The trends to know in 2019

- GOOD OLD GAMES (GOG)
- WeGame[9] from Tencent
- Nitro from Discord

The best-known and most popular online platform for selling PC games is Steam, so we'll be using data from this store from here on out.

The trend chart was compiled in accordance with the data presented on Steam[10]—as a basis for this, we used the chart showing the popularity of languages among game developers who have published games on Steam and compared this data to the languages chosen by users as their primary language[11]:

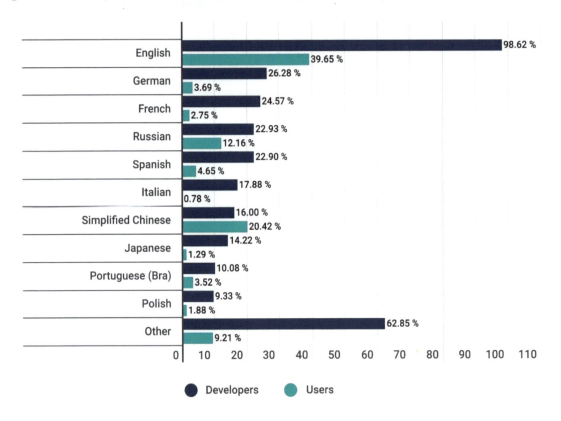

The difference in the popularity of Chinese among users and developers is especially striking.

The latest data on the distribution of Steam's revenue by country is only for 2017—at this point, Valve earned[12] USD 4.3 billion from game sales on the platform, 34% of which came from North American players:

[9] Tencent WeGame

[10] Languages of games on Steam, Nimdzi and Konstantin Dranch The selection includes over 26,000 games. The total is greater than 100% because many games are localized into multiple languages.

[11] Data on Users' Hardware and Software, September 2019

[12] Distribution of Steam sales revenue worldwide as of August 2017, by region GeekWire.

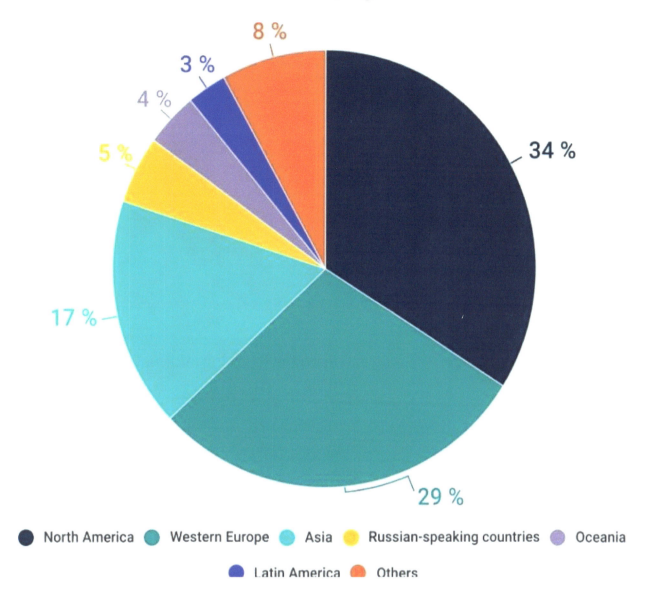

Steam revenue, August 2017

● North America ● Western Europe ● Asia ● Russian-speaking countries ● Oceania
● Latin America ● Others

Markets in which releasing PC games makes sense include China, the USA, and Western and Eastern Europe.

To evaluate your game's prospects in these markets, you can use data from SteamSpy:

1. Choose a few games from the same genre as yours, i.e. your competitors.
2. See which languages they've been localized into and how much money they make in each country.
3. Identify your place among your competitors and act.

For online games, you can use statistics for the distribution of online languages[13]:

_____

[13]Internet Users by Language April 30, 2019.

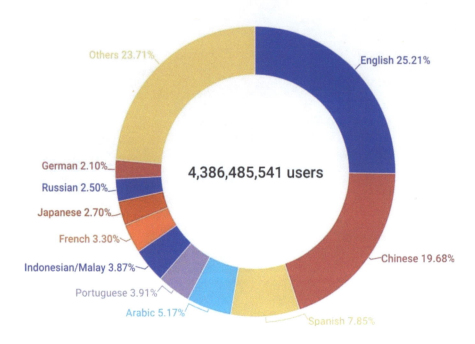

Internet users by language, April 30, 2019

Using various online services[14], you can learn the following information about your competitors:

- Traffic volume
- Traffic sources
- Traffic distribution by advertising network
- Top 5 referral websites
- Top 5 keywords
- Trajectory data and behavioral factors

As for genres, action adventure games and shooters remain the most popular genres on PC and consoles—as well as variations of MMORPGs depending on the country. Games from specific subgenres also gain popularity from time to time—recently this has included multiplayer online battle arena (MOBA) and battle royale games.

1.3. Choosing Markets for Mobile Games

As of now, the mobile games market still has low barriers to entry and is fairly transparent in comparison to that of PC and console games, as there is a far more abundant wealth of data and metrics available for analysis. However, the general rule of thumb[15] remains the same for any segment: the amount of profit you make off each player must be three times greater than the cost of engaging said player (LTV[16] > 3 x CAC).

---

[14] For example, SimilarWeb.com
[15] Market selection for mobile games using a localization ROI model
[16] You can learn more about LTV and other metrics at Devtodev.

Female mobile gamers slightly exceed males within the same category in number and generally prefer puzzle games (match 3 games, farming simulators, etc.). It is also important to note that game genres often undergo evolution, so for instance, certain hidden object games may include a match 3 quest and vice versa[17].

Personas by gender
Among mobile-first gamers, 2019

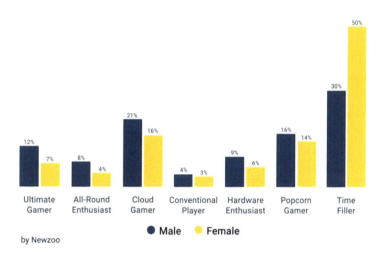

by Newzoo

Besides the gender-associated preferences, different game genres, subgenres, and settings enjoy a varying degree of popularity depending on the country. Furthermore, the corresponding predilections of these audiences may also change over time.

Top games by Smartphone MAU, 2018

	Brazil	Canada	China	France	Germany	India	Japan	South Korea	US	UK
1	Free Fire	Candy Crush Saga	Anipop	Candy Crush Saga	QuizClash	Ludo King	Disney Tsum Tsum	PUBG MOBILE	Pokemon GO	Candy Crush Saga
2	CandyCrush Saga	Pokemon GO	Honour of Kings	Clash Royale	Candy Crush Saga	Candy Crush Saga	Monster Strike	Clash Royale	Candy Crush Saga	Helix Jump
3	Helix Jump	HQ - Live Trivia Game Show	PUBG: Exciting Battlefield	Pokemon GO	Pokemon GO	PUBG MOBILE	Pokemon GO	Rider	New Words With Friends	Pokemon GO
4	Cartola FC Oficial	Helix Jump	Landlord Poker	FDJ	Helix Jump	Clash of Clans	Puzzle & Dragons	Pmang New Matgo	HQ - Live Trivia Game Show	8 Ball Pool
5	Clash Royale	Wordscapes	Mini World Block Art	Clash of Clans	Clash Royale	Doodle Army 2: Mini Militia	Knives Out	Everybody's Marble	Helix Jump	Mobility Ware Solitaire

by App Annie

[17] 20 Mobile Gaming Statistics That Will Blow You Away

According to the 2018 data, this is what the mobile game markets look like by volume for different languages:

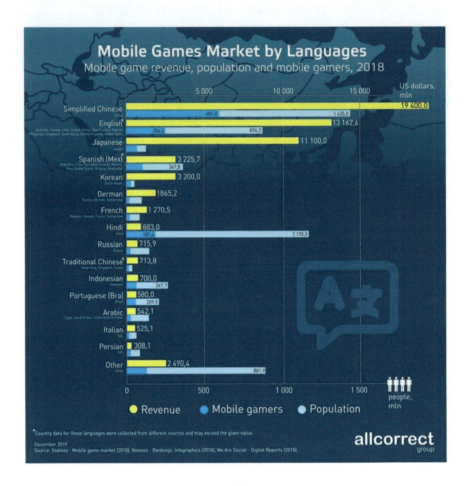

Moreover, the cost of attracting a new user[18] and the profit a developer can potentially make off them varies depending on the said player's country and the game in question. According to our data, 2-10% of total spendings on culture, art, and entertainment[19] are on mobile games. Additionally, the higher the share of rural population in country, the higher the share of expenditures on mobile games—this is most likely explained by the fact that there aren't many available alternative sources of entertainment.

In 2017, we went to analyze mobile RPGs so that we could draw a conclusion as to whether the payback period of a game localization is affected by a specific market it is released in and by how much. You can familiarize yourself with the results in greater detail in our article[20]. To summarize it all, these are the interesting facts we learnt from the research:

---

[18]Mobile Gaming Apps Report 2019 User Acquisition Trends And Benchmarks.
[19]UN Classification.
[20]Market selection for mobile games using a localization ROI model. Gala

1. The number of downloads and revenue across a selection of 300 games (out of 32,000) localized into 11 languages and released in 11 countries are log-normally distributed.

2. The number of downloads across all RPG games is log-normally distributed as well.

3. Our research has allowed to draw a tangential conclusion that localized RPG games on average generate profits that are twice as high as unlocalized games (but this does not necessarily imply causality). This is confirmed by data from Google (x1.9 increase for strategy and RPG games) and unpublished data we received from our clients.

As a result, we derived a formula that can be used to calculate the ROI of a localization, and created our personal tool for making such calculations.

allcorrect group	Platform's fee	# of words in game	% of installs paid	ROLI sigma taking into the account given expences per country and platform fee			
	30%	13000	50%	C1	C2	C3	C4
Language	average loc rate	cost of loc	CPI	ROLI C1	ROLI C2	ROLI C3	ROLI C4
Afrikaans	0,1700	2210	0,69	51%	-86%	-97%	-99%
Arabic	0,1400	1820	0,22	21381%	1934%	-4%	-37%
Bokmål	0,1800	2340	1,05	417%	203%	-135%	-117%
Czech	0,1400	1820	0,31	2040%	479%	-121%	-106%
Danish	0,1800	2340	0,87	342%	-50%	-131%	-114%
Dutch	0,1800	2340	0,60	4005%	-111%	-94%	-101%
English	0,1500	1950	0,49	445363%	8194%	-1161%	-270%
Finnish	0,1800	2340	0,71	1209%	-130%	-112%	-103%
French	0,1400	1820	0,71	7673%	1144%	-51%	-109%
German	0,1400	1820	0,75	17732%	1988%	8%	-110%
Hebrew	0,1800	2340	0,36	-857%	-198%	-122%	-111%
Hindi	0,1400	1820	0,13	496%	-78%	-79%	-97%
Hungarian	0,1400	1820	0,20	1547%	-138%	-115%	-107%
Indonesian	0,1400	1820	0,14	3728%	106%	-64%	-98%
Italian	0,1400	1820	0,29	2777%	-8%	20%	-106%
Japanese	0,1400	1820	1,99	186565%	4911%	43%	-168%
Korean	0,1400	1820	0,46	6329%	411%	-80%	-108%
Malay	0,1400	1820	0,32	1252%	54%	55%	-92%
Polish	0,1400	1820	0,24	1608%	383%	-96%	-109%
Portuguese	0,1400	1820	0,11	3636%	9%	-95%	-109%
Romanian	0,1700	2210	0,13	-498%	118%	-110%	-108%
Russian	0,1350	1755	0,20	22793%	1659%	291%	-77%
	Made for:				By:	Allcorrect	

Knowing the percentage share of paid installations, their cost, and cost of localization, we can predict which language localizations have a payback period of a year or less.

We began employing a similar approach before even developing the tool—as it had turned out, treating a game localization in the same way as purchasing traffic volume may result in a 1,890% ROI in as little as half a year[21].

---

[21] A 1.890% localization ROI in six months and other secrets of the mobile RPG-games market

2. Age Ratings for Games

Age ratings for video games first appeared in the USA. In 1994 major game publishers and developers created a noncommercial self-regulating agency called the ESRB[22] and developed a system of age ratings for games similar to that used by the movie industry. This was eventually followed by the establishment of PEGI and others.

There are currently over 15 organizations in the world[23] that assign age ratings to video games.

When an age rating is assigned to a video game, the presence or absence of the following factors is typically considered[24]:
- Smoking, and use of alcohol, drugs, or other prohibited addictive substances
- Violence
- Depictions of criminal activity
- Depictions of blood, mutation, and cannibalism
- Use of profane language
- Depiction of sex and sexual corruption
- Gambling
- Horror imagery
- Online interaction with other players
- User-generated content

In addition to the game itself, a rating may also have to be assigned separately to:
- Game demos
- Game trailers (advertising videos)
- Any potential expansions

At the moment, if you wish to release a game on consoles, mobile app stores, such as the App Store, Google Play, the Amazon Store, and a few others, and on physical media it is required by law in most countries that it has an age rating assigned to it.

This procedure isn't mandatory for releasing PC games online (on Steam, GOG, the Epic Games Store, etc.) as of yet[25], but we think this is going to change in the near future.

Online games do not get assigned age ratings in all countries, but you can also expect this to change in the next few years—among other things, the appearance of player identification systems and restrictions on in-game player time similar to that used in South Korea[26] should be accounted for.

---

[22]Entertainment Software Rating Board
[23]From the ESRB to RARS: Who Rates Video Games and how They Do It
[24]Indonesia Game Rating System
[25]Console Indie Development in Russian Provinces.
[26]Five Years in Jail for Cheat Codes: Why the South Korean Government is Making Video Game Laws Harsher

All in all, the video game age rating system is becoming more regulated and universal, while the procedure for getting a rating is growing ever simpler.

The principles by which particular age ratings are assigned can be divided into three conceptual segments. These in turn are divided based on the rules for determining what is permitted or prohibited:
1.   The United States and Europe. Discrimination based on gender, race, or sexual orientation is prohibited. The primary rating boards are the ESRB and PEGI.
2.   Muslim countries. Religious prohibitions are widespread, including a prohibition against the positive representation of homosexuality, as well as nudity and depiction of alcohol, gambling, gods and prophets, heaven and hell, etc.
3.   Asia, including Southeastern Asia. Extreme violence is prohibited, as is depiction of blood and human corpses, portrayal of the country's history in a negative cultural context, etc. Local rating systems or the Taiwanese system (the KP) are in place.

Russia's rating system is currently a combination of those used in European and Muslim countries—the acceptable level of violence is similar to that in the USA and Western Europe, but as in Muslim and certain Asian countries, positive depictions of homosexuality are prohibited.

Country/System	0/1	2	3	4	5	6	7	8	9	10	11	12	13	14	15	16	17	18	19	20	21	Other	Assignment procedure	Cost	Restrictions	Notes
App Store (iOS)				4+ (5 y/o or less)		4+ (6-8 y/o)			9+ / 4+ (9-11 y/o)			12+					17+					No Rating	The form is filled in independently	Free	Gambling, high level of violence, sexual exploitation, graphic image of sex, discrimination based on race, sex, or sexual orientation	Required for all App Store apps.
ESRB (Canada, Mexico, USA)					EC					E10+			T				M	AO				RP (Rating pending)	Committee	USD 0-12,500	Discrimination by race, gender or sexual orientation	Confederate flag is prohibited in games in USA.
Generalized IARC (Google Play, Nintendo eShop, Microsoft Store, Oculus VR store, and some others)			3				7					12				16				18		no	The form is filled in independently	Free	Sexual exploitation, graphic image of sex, discrimination based on race, sex, or sexual orientation, etc.	Required for all Google Play apps and other aforementioned online platforms.
PEGI (EU, UK, Canada (Quebec), India, Israel, Pakistan, South Africa)			3				7					12				16		18				no	The form is filled in independently and then selectively inspected by the committee	EUR 450-1,100-2,200-2,800 for one platform	Discrimination by race, gender or sexual orientation	
Australia (ACB)								G			PG				M	MA15+		R18+				RC (blocked) / CTC (rating pending)	Committee	USD 300-400	Gambling, high level of violence, sexual exploitation, graphic image of sex, discrimination based on race, sex, or sexual orientation	
Argentina (INCAA)							ATR								+13				+18				Independently	Free		Almost never used
Brazil (ClassInd)					L					10		12		14		16		18				no	Independently	Free	Accept PEGI; IARC is required for digitally released games and apps	
Germany (USK)			0			6			12							16		18		No labelling		Prohibited	Committee	EUR 1,200 + 300 additional platform + 300 trailer	Realistic depiction of human death of people, human corpses, image of the Third Reich symbols outside the scientific context	Games with pending rating are to be sold only to adults until the rating is received.

Country/System	0/1	2	3	4	5	6	7	8	9	10	11	12	13	14	15	16	17	18	19	20	21	Other	Assignment procedure	Cost	Restrictions	Notes
Indonesia (IGRS)	SU		3+				7+						13+					18+				no	Independently	Free	Depictions of human genitalia, buttocks, female breasts, sex, sounds indicative of a sexual act, gambling, extremely realistic horror.	
Iran			+3				+7					+12			+15			+18				no	Committee	Free	Games with depictions of intense violence, nudity (especially female nudity) and sex, references to gods and prophets, heaven or hell, depictions of alcoholic beverages and their consumption, or gambling are prohibited.	Ratings are only assigned to PC and mobile games, since console games are banned in Iran.
New Zealand						G						PG	R13		R15	R16	M	R18				Prohibited	Committee	USD 1,400-1,500	High level of violence, sexual exploitation, graphic image of sex, discrimination based on race, sex, or sexual orientation	Australian classification for games rated G, PG, and R18 may be used.
United Arab Emirates	Нет		3				7					12				16		18				no	The form is filled in independently and then selectively inspected by the committee		References to gods or prophets	
Portugal (modified PEGI)				4		6						12				16		18				no			Discrimination based on gender or sexual orientation	A slightly modified version of PEGI is used.
Russia			0+			6+						12+				16+		18+				no	Independently	Free	Positive depictions of homosexuality are prohibited for children, as are symbols of proscribed terrorist groups or organizations (ISIS and others) and misrepresentation of military conflicts that contradicts the official news (Syria and others).	Russia has its own rating system but has no governing body assigning age ratings to games. The rating is assigned by the developers themselves. PEGI and ESRB are also used.
Saudi Arabia	Нет		3				7					12				16		18				no			References to gods or prophets	

Country/System	0/1	2	3	4	5	6	7	8	9	10	11	12	13	14	15	16	17	18	19	20	21	Other	Assignment procedure	Cost	Restrictions	Notes
Singapore (IMDA)	General															Age advisory		M18				Prohibited	The form is filled in independently, and then the committee assigns a corresponding rating	Free	Undermining of social system and values, discrimination based on race or religion, incitement of conflicts based on racial or religious grounds, etc.	
Taiwan (GSRMR)	普通 (G)					保護 (P)						輔12 (PG 12)			輔15 (PG 15)			限制 (R)				No	Committee	Free		Children above the age of 6 are allowed to play Nintendo 3DS games. De facto, the rating system is used in Southeast Asia, including Hong Kong.
South Korea (GRAC)	ALL											12			15			18				Classification rejected	Committee	USD 1,000-1,500	Realistic killings and blood in games	In Korea, developers of online games are required to identify their users and control the time they spend playing their games.
Japan (CERO)	A											B			C		D	Z				審査予定 (Rating pending)	Committee	USD 1,000	Depictions of human genitalia	There are two governing bodies in Japan that assign age ratings to games: CERO and EOCS. Games intended for adults can have their rating assigned by EOCS.

White—No restrictions: For any age / For children / No rating

Yellow—No restrictions: Parental consent desirable

Purple—No restrictions: Not restricted but not recommended for children

Red—Restricted: Parental consent required

Black—Prohibited: Adults only / Age-restricted / Prohibited

2.1. Examples of Game Ratings Based on Various Rating Systems

How do rating systems work in practice? The easiest way to answer this question is to provide examples of real ratings of well-known games in different countries[27]:

System/Country	Game rating	
	Sims 4	Pokemon X and Y
ESRB (USA, Canada, Mexico)	T (a moderate degree of sexual content is permitted)	E
PEGI (Europe)	12 (unrealistic violence and nudity are permitted, as is profanity outside of a sexual context)	7 (unrealistic violence is permitted)
ACB (Australia)	M	PG (violence)
ClassInd[28] (Brazil)	16 (sex, simulation of virtual relationships)	no rating
USK (Germany)	6+	0+
RARS (Russia)	18+ (the player can choose a character of the same gender as their own character as a partner)	6+
GSRMR[29] (Taiwan, Southeast Asia)	PG15 (sex, violence, virtual romance)	P (violence)

The concept of acceptable levels of violence and sexual context for different age groups in different countries can vary significantly depending on local laws and traditions.

---

[27] How Video Game Age Classifications Vary by Country
[28] Database of Age Codes for Video Games in Brazil
[29] Taiwan Entertainment Software Rating Information

3. Processing Personal Data

3.1. Processing Personal Data in EU Countries

In 2018, the European Union enacted the General Data Protection Regulation, known as GDPR, which is designed to give EU citizens an opportunity to control over their personal data. If you accept payments from citizens from any country of the European Union, if EU citizens can register for your game, or if you use any type of analytics or user identification systems, then you are subject to GDPR.

How to comply[30] with these regulations? See the key points below:

1. Create a publicly available policy[31] on processing of personal data. This policy should make it clear to the average user what data is being processed, how it is done, for what purpose, and how long it will take. Personal data cannot be stored for longer than is necessary for its purpose (Art. 5 of the GDPR).

2. Create a publicly available policy on personal data storage (Data Retention Policy).

3. You must either provide users with the opportunity to refuse having their personal data processed, or destroy it. Additionally, you are required to describe the users' right to manage their personal data. (Art. 15–18 of the GDPR).

4. Explain how the data will be protected. A Compliance & Security document is optional, but it's best to have a resource that details how you protect user data.

5. Inform users if you send their data to other countries (International transfers of your personal data) Art. 45 of the GDPR.

6. Provide contact information, including your legal address, and the contact information of your Data Protection Officer if you have one.

7. If your game is rated for ages 16 and under, you must add a feature where users can select their age at registration and, for those younger than 16, indicate that they have obtained parental consent. Art. 8 of the GDPR.

8. Create publicly available Payment and Cookie Policies[32] that outline your payment processes and what cookies your system uses.

9. Users must expressly consent to having their personal data processed as described in your personal data processing policy.

In practice, this means that you must add an agreement window that appears during user registration and details your terms of use, payment policy, cookie policy, and policies on personal data processing and protection (according to the regulation, consent to processing of personal data must be a separate document. All other policies and rules can be combined into one document for convenience). Follow the rules you have set and notify the appropriate authorities[33] within 72 hours in the event of a data leak.

---

[30] GDPR & Data Protection Documents
[31] GDPR Privacy Notice Template
[32] Cookie Consent Management
[33] European Data Protection Board

26

You should also ensure that all third-party services in your games comply with the GDPR. There are also a number of reasons why it is best to store and process personal data from European users within a European jurisdiction and not send it to third parties.

There are generators that create security policies[34] and user agreements for applications. You may use these as templates to make the required documents.

Here are your liability risks should you fail to comply with the law:

1.   A fine of up to 10 million euros or 2% of the firm's worldwide annual revenue from the preceding financial year (whichever is more) will be applied on the controller, processor, or responsible control/certification organization that fails to meet their obligations.

2.   A fine of up to 20 million euros or 4% of the firm's worldwide annual revenue from the preceding financial year (whichever is more) will be applied on the controller that violates the rules for processing of personal data. This includes processing a user's personal data without his or her consent, violating the rights of data subjects, or transferring personal data to a recipient in another country who is not GDPR compliant.

3.2. Processing Personal Data in Russia

The rules under federal law 152-FZ for processing the personal data of Russian citizens are much like those for European citizens[35]. You could even say they are easier to follow overall and, in some ways, are more logical than the EU's rules.

Russia's policy on the processing of personal data[36] can be integrated with other rules. You cannot receive a copy of your personal data or send it to another service. There is also no need to get parental consent in games intended for children.

It is a good idea to process personal data only for the purposes of fulfilling a specific contract with a specific individual. Disseminating or distributing the data in any other way would require you to register as a personal data controller with Roskomnadzor (the Federal Service for Supervision of Communications, Information Technology and Mass Media) [37].

The personal data of Russian users must also be processed and stored only in Russia.

One particular distinction of this law is that you must be able to confirm receipt of users' consent to the processing of their personal data.

---

[34] App Privacy Policy Generator
[35] GDPR: Complying with the Obligations
[36] Policy on the Processing of Personal Data
[37] Complying with 152-FZ Federal Law on Data Protection

Violation of the 152-FZ, depending on who did it and how, will result in a fine of up to 300,000 rubles or full compensation to injured parties for damages[38].

3.3. Processing Personal Data in Other Countries

As of yet, there are no laws on the processing of personal data in other countries, though the US state of California will see a similar law come into effect in 2020[39]. So, for now, you can consult the GDPR.

[38]Liability for Breaking the Law on Personal Data
[39]California's New Data Privacy Law Offers Strongest Internet User Protection in the USA

4. Culturalization

Culturalization is the process of amending a video game with consideration for the mentality of the target region population. It makes the product comprehensible and gives the players an opportunity to enjoy the gameplay more.

There are two types of cultural adaptation of gaming products for regional markets:
• Reactive culturalization includes identifying and removing elements which may prompt users to quit playing the game.
• Proactive culturalization includes identifying and adding to a game culture-specific traits and elements pervasive in that particular region.

The first type helps to avoid financial loss due to a game being perceived negatively, while the second helps to establish a loyal player community.

This guide contains a brief overview on the culture-specific traits of target audiences in 28 countries.

The data sources are presented in the tables in the appendix and in the notes.

The order of countries with infographics follows. The countries highlighted in green are the ones having a slide on culturalization.

4.1. China[40]

Market size

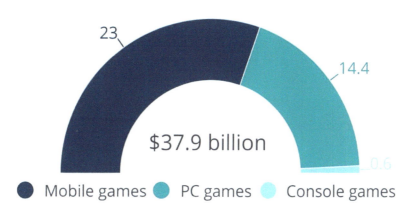

23

14.4

$37.9 billion

0.6

● Mobile games ● PC games ● Console games

Players' spending

Average spending for recreation and culture — $398

Average spending for games — $61.25

Average spending for mobile games — $32.28

54% use e-wallets to pay

94%

of paying gamers spent money on in-game items or virtual goods in the past 6 months

60%

of women and 55% of men bought cosmetics/skins

51.94%

low English fluency according to EF EPI index

0.2%

fraud rate and 0.1% chargeback rate

---

[40]Distribution of players by age and gender, including data on mobile gamers taken from Newzoo reports.

Population of China

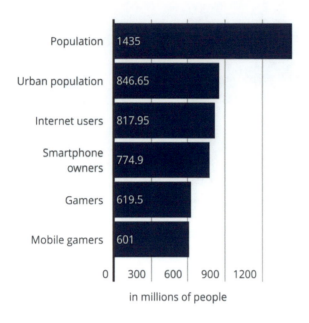

	in millions of people
Population	1435
Urban population	846.65
Internet users	817.95
Smartphone owners	774.9
Gamers	619.5
Mobile gamers	601

Number of gamers in China

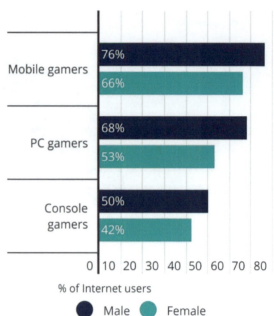

% of Internet users

	Male	Female
Mobile gamers	76%	66%
PC gamers	68%	53%
Console gamers	50%	42%

● Male ● Female

FACTS ABOUT GAMERS

Age and gender distribution

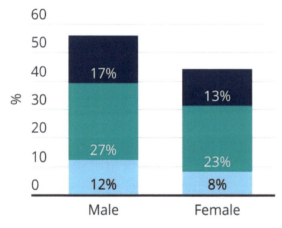

	Male	Female
36–60 y/o	17%	13%
21–35 y/o	27%	23%
10–20 y/o	12%	8%

● 10–20 y/o ● 21–35 y/o ● 36–60 y/o

Popular mobile game genres

№	By revenue	By number of downloads
1	RPG	Action
2	Action	RPG
3	Strategy	Strategy

76.9%

of players use Android smartphones and tablets, and 22.2% of players use iOS

11 GB

people in China use this amount of mobile traffic in average yearly, while the average Internet speed is 33.72 Mbit/s

8.11%

the percentage of average consumer spending per capita for recreation and culture made up by mobile games in China

$1.32

is the average user acquisition cost for a mobile game

Chinese Culture

Language: Standard Chinese
National symbols: red five-star flag; coat of arms with an image of the Gate of Heavenly Peace and five stars against a red background; anthem is "March of the Volunteers"; the outline of the country on maps (resembles a huge bird soaring in the sky).
Other important cultural elements: rice, dragons, Temple of Heavenly Peace, calligraphy, traditional music.

 Main holidays (nonpublic holidays are <u>underlined</u>):
Chinese New Year (January–February, depending on the lunar calendar), Tomb Sweeping Day (April), Dragon Boat Festival (June), Qixi Festival (August), Mid-Autumn Festival (September), National Day (October 1st-8th), <u>Singles' Day (November 11th, shopping holiday popular among young Chinese people)</u>.

Color associations

Symbol of happiness and everything good	Cannot be worn as a headdress color; this means the wearer was deceived (usually means the person is a cuckold)	It has long been the color of mourning, but ceases to bear this meaning

Animal associations

Cute	Contrary to the stereotypes, are not food	Stupid

Objectionable or forbidden symbols: images of traditional Chinese objects and national symbols depicted in a negative light, poppies (flowers) because of their association with drugs, religious symbolism (especially Muslim), swastikas, communist emblems and symbols, Winnie the Pooh (because he looks like Xi Jinping, Secretary General of the Chinese Communist Party).

Objectionable or forbidden themes: religion, politics, and communism. Best not to joke about China's history or reference the country's leaders in any way.

41

---

[41]From here onwards, the data on color semiotics is taken from Localizing Images: Cultural Aspects and Visual Metaphors and supplemented by a survey of Allcorrect translators. The data on animal associations is obtained by a survey of Allcorrect translators. The data on holidays and days off is taken from OfficeHolidays. The data on the most popular smartphone manufacturers, mobile operating systems, search engines, and social networks is taken from Statcounter as 2018 average values, while the data on the most popular messengers comes from Messengerpeople. The data on restrictions, prohibitions, and sensitive information in games comes from the guidelines of corresponding rating committees, as well as requirements and recommendations of the game companies that are Allcorrect's clients.

Culturalization Case
Game: Billiards simulator

Problem: Some landmarks on the Beijing map didn't look true Chinese.

Solution: Minor fixes of graphical objects were introduced to match the atmosphere of China.

BEFORE
The garden decorations were more of Japanese style.

AFTER
Japanese-looking elements with red roof removed.

BEFORE

The stone lions should be in pair, and two lions should be put at the opposite positions of the corners of the stairs (empty circles).

AFTER

Lions put at both sides of the entrance.

4.2. Hong Kong[42]

Market size

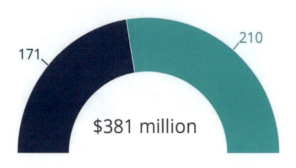

171   210

$381 million

● Mobile games ● PC/console games

Players' spending

Average spending for recreation and culture	$2008
Average spending for games	$41
Average spending for mobile games	$25

49%
use bank cards

76%

of gamers are willing to pay for better Internet plans versus 45% of non-gamers

42%

of gamers use YouTube to watch music videos

56.38%

average English fluency according to the EF EPI index

27.44%

of gamers purchase less than 1 game a month, while 1.82% purchase more than 10 games a month

---

[42]Distribution of players by age and gender, including data on mobile gamers taken from Newzoo reports.

Population of Hong Kong

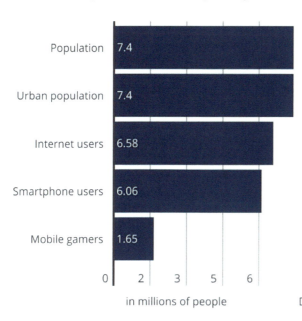

	in millions of people
Population	7.4
Urban population	7.4
Internet users	6.58
Smartphone users	6.06
Mobile gamers	1.65

in millions of people

Number of gamers in Hong Kong

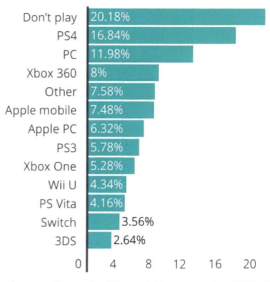

Don't play	20.18%
PS4	16.84%
PC	11.98%
Xbox 360	8%
Other	7.58%
Apple mobile	7.48%
Apple PC	6.32%
PS3	5.78%
Xbox One	5.28%
Wii U	4.34%
PS Vita	4.16%
Switch	3.56%
3DS	2.64%

Details: Hong Kong; Cint (Cint Insight Exchange); 4,999*; 18+ y/o

FACTS ABOUT GAMERS

Age and gender distribution

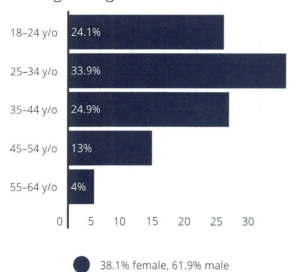

18–24 y/o	24.1%
25–34 y/o	33.9%
35–44 y/o	24.9%
45–54 y/o	13%
55–64 y/o	4%

● 38.1% female, 61.9% male

Popular mobile game genres

№	By revenue	By number of downloads
1	Sport	Adventure
2	Battler	Action
3	RPG	Hyper Casual

Source: Datamagic

54.60%

of players use iOS smartphones and tablets, 44.98% — Android users

242 GB

of mobile traffic is used in Hong Kong by a person in average yearly, while the Internet speed is 32.26 Mbit/s

1.26%

the percentage of average consumer spending per capita for recreation and culture made up by mobile games in Hong Kong

$0.90

is the average user acquisition cost for a mobile game

Hong Kong Culture

Language: Chinese.

National symbols: red flag with a white stylized image of a five-petaled Bauhinia; coat of arms with similar elements in a round frame; anthem is the "March of the Volunteers".

Other important cultural elements: skyscrapers, red taxis, double buses, feng shui, china (porcelain), guohua painting.

Main holidays:
New Year's Day (January 1st), Chinese Lunar New Year (It usually has the date falling in January or February in the Gregorian calendar), Ching Ming Festival or Tomb Sweeping Day, (March or April), Easter (April 10th-13th), Buddha's Birthday (April or May), Dragon Boat Festival (June or July), Special Administration Region (SAR) Day (July 1st), Mid-Autumn Festival (Septemder or Ocrober), Chung Yeung Festival (October or November), Christmas (December 25th). The dates for most holidays are dependent on the lunar calendar.

Color associations

Negative colors

Positive colors

Animal associations

Masters of the water, imply strength

Warrior's symbol

Appear in images associated with colonial Hong Kong

Objectionable content: deformed imagery of the flag, coat of arms, or religious symbols; images of alcohol or tobacco use in games targeted at persons under 18.

Objectionable or forbidden themes: Chinese law and politics, censorship in Hong Kong.

Top on mobile market in Hong Kong

device

OS

4.3. Taiwan

Market size

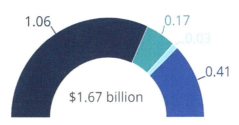

1.06   0.17   0.03   0.41

$1.67 billion

● Mobile games ● Browser games ● Console games
● Online PC games

Players' spending

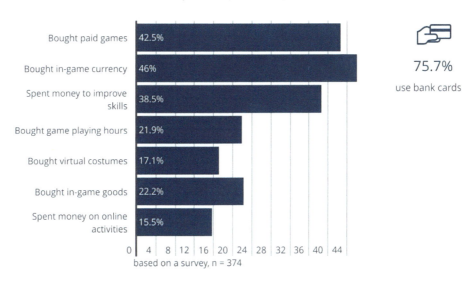

Bought paid games	42.5%
Bought in-game currency	46%
Spent money to improve skills	38.5%
Bought game playing hours	21.9%
Bought virtual costumes	17.1%
Bought in-game goods	22.2%
Spent money on online activities	15.5%

0 4 8 12 16 20 24 28 32 36 40 44

based on a survey, n = 374

75.7%

use bank cards

80.5%

of online users who watch gaming stream content use YouTube, and 22.5% use Twitch

21.5%

of male game spenders and 13.2% of female game spenders use ATMs to pay for gaming content

44.1%

of game spenders consider game type the biggest influence of their in-game purchases, and 42.8% consider discounts the key influence

51.88%

low English fluency according to the EF EPI index

Population of Taiwan

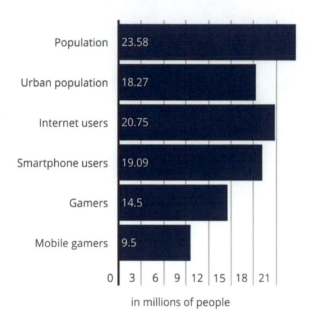

	in millions of people
Population	23.58
Urban population	18.27
Internet users	20.75
Smartphone users	19.09
Gamers	14.5
Mobile gamers	9.5

in millions of people

Number of gamers in Taiwan

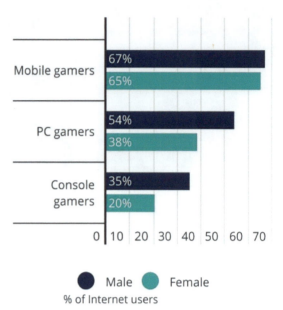

	Male	Female
Mobile gamers	67%	65%
PC gamers	54%	38%
Console gamers	35%	20%

● Male ● Female

% of Internet users

FACTS ABOUT GAMERS

Age and gender distribution

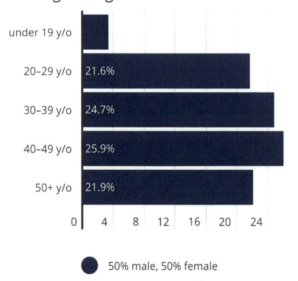

under 19 y/o	
20–29 y/o	21.6%
30–39 y/o	24.7%
40–49 y/o	25.9%
50+ y/o	21.9%

● 50% male, 50% female

51.88%

of players use iOS smartphones and
tablets, 47.87% of players use Android

43.49 Mbit/s

is the average Internet speed in
Taiwan, and $9.49 is the average cost
of 1 GB of Internet traffic

54%

of online users watch gaming video
content (49% of them watch it on their
mobile devices)

Popular mobile game genres

№	By revenue	By number of downloads
1	Action: RPG	Action: RPG
2	MOBA	Action: Arcade
3	Slots	Match-3

Source: Datamagic

$0.83

is the average user acquisition cost for
a mobile game

Taiwanese Culture

Language: Chinese Mandarin.

National symbols: red flag with a white sun against a dark blue sky; coat of arms in the form of a blue circle with a white 12-point sun; national anthem of the Republic of China.

Other important cultural elements: skyscrapers, lakes, puppet theater, electro-techno, night markets.

 Main holidays (nonpublic holidays are <u>underlined</u>):
Republic Day (January 1st), Chinese New Year (January–February, depending on the lunar calendar), <u>Lantern Festival (February or March)</u>, Peace Memorial Day (February or March), Ching Ming Festival Holiday (April 2nd-5th), Labour Day (May 1st), Dragon Boat Festival (June), Mid Autumn Festival (September-October), National Day (October 10th), <u>Double Ninth Day or Chung Yeung Festival (October)</u>.

Color associations

Death

Animal associations

Taiwanese black bear is the nation's symbol and is considered to be strong

Cute

Objectionable content: religious symbols, images of a deformed flag and coat of arms. Taiwan is actually rather comfortable with the swastika. Here it is not associated with Nazism, as it is an ancient image of the sun, movement and life.

Forbidden subjects: Taiwan's political status and the anti-government protests called "Incident 228" which took place on February 28th, 1947, and led to mass casualties.

Top brands on mobile market in Taiwan

device   OS

4.4. Singapore

Market size

288.2

41.8

$330 million

● Mobile games   ● PC and console games

Players' spending

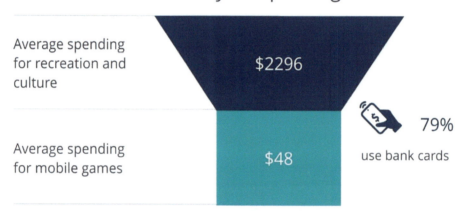

Average spending for recreation and culture	$2296
Average spending for mobile games	$48

79%
use bank cards

 38%

of gamers would quit their jobs to become a professional video gamer

 3.8%

of gamers play more than 15 hours a week, 19.6% play 1–3 hours a week, 25.8%—less than 1 hour a week

 68.63%

very high English fluency according to the EF EPI index

 46%

of users use WhatsApp as a messenger

Population of Singapore

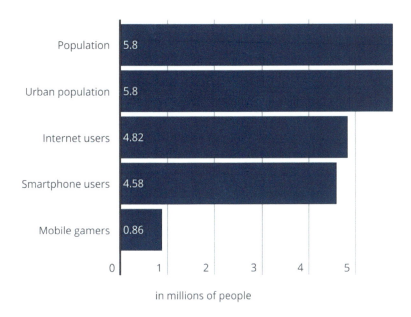

	in millions of people
Population	5.8
Urban population	5.8
Internet users	4.82
Smartphone users	4.58
Mobile gamers	0.86

in millions of people

FACTS ABOUT GAMERS

Age and gender distribution

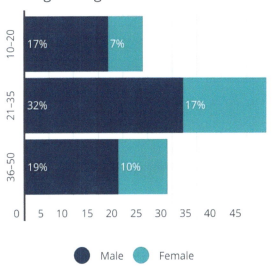

● Male   ● Female

Popular mobile game genres

№	By revenue	By number of downloads
1	RPG	RPG
2	Shooter	Match-3
3	Strategy	Battle Royale

Source: Datamagic

76.73%

of players use Android smartphones and tablets, and 15.38% use iOS

115.8 GB

of mobile traffic is used in Singapore by a person in average yearly, while the Internet speed is 53.47 Mbit/s

2.12%

the percentage of average consumer spending per capita for recreation and culture made up by mobile games in Singapore

$0.63

is the average user acquisition cost for a mobile game

4.5. Japan

Market size

335.21

896.71

$1,231.92 million

● Mobile games ● PC/console games

Players' spending

Average spending for recreation and culture	$1560
Average spending for games	$284.48
Average spending for mobile games	$189.42

65%
use bank cards

 77%
of paying gamers spent money on in-game items or virtual goods in the past 6 months

 47%
of men and 27% of women bought DLC/expansion packs

 37%
of mobile gamers live with parents

 51.8%
low English fluency according to the EF EPI index

 0.1%
fraud rate

Population of Japan

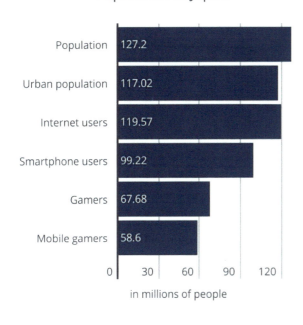

	in millions of people
Population	127.2
Urban population	117.02
Internet users	119.57
Smartphone users	99.22
Gamers	67.68
Mobile gamers	58.6

Number of gamers in Japan

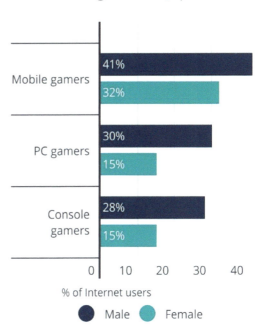

% of Internet users

	Male	Female
Mobile gamers	41%	32%
PC gamers	30%	15%
Console gamers	28%	15%

● Male ● Female

FACTS ABOUT MOBILE GAMERS

Age and gender distribution

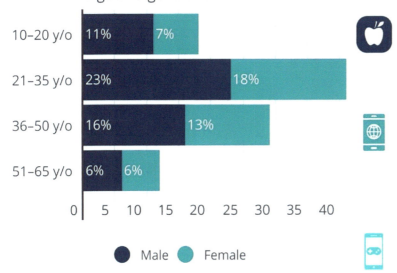

	Male	Female
10–20 y/o	11%	7%
21–35 y/o	23%	18%
36–50 y/o	16%	13%
51–65 y/o	6%	6%

● Male ● Female

61.98%

of players use iOS smartphones and tablets, 37.82% of players use Android

102.52 GB

of mobile traffic is used in Japan by a person in average yearly, while the Internet speed is 30.85 Mbit/s

12.4%

the percentage of average consumer spending per capita for recreation and culture made up by mobile games in Japan

$5.35

is the average user acquisition cost for a mobile game

Top iOS game genres

№	By revenue	By number of downloads
1	Role playng	Action
2	Action	Puzzle
3	Adventure	Adventure

Source: Newzoo

Japanese Culture

Language: Japanese.

National symbols: white flag with a large red circle at its center; the imperial seal is a 16-petal chrysanthemum; the anthem is "Kimigayo".

Other important cultural elements: ninjas, geishas, harakiri, kamikaze, samurai, origami, ikebana, calligraphy, traditional theater (Kabuki and Bunraku), anime and manga.

Main holidays:
New Year (January 1st), Coming-of-age Day (2nd Monday of January), National Fondation Day (February 11st), Vernal Equinox Day (March 20th or 21th), Golden Week (April 29th - May 6th), Marine Day (3rd Monday of July), Moumtain Day (August 11st-12nd), Obon (August 13th-15th, not a public holiday), Respect of the Aged Day (3rd Monday of September), Autumnal Equinox Day (September 23rd), Health-Sports Day (2nd Monday of October), The Emperor's Coronation (October 22nd), Culture Day (November 3rd-4th), Labour Thanksgiving Day (November 23rd or following Monday if it falls on a Sunday)

Color associations

Unhappy, funeral

Happy

Animal associations

Stupid

A kind of mascot of a shrine

Objectionable content: chrysanthemum images (associated with funerals). One of the symbols of Buddhism is the swastika, so it is important to point it in the correct direction.

Objectionable or forbidden themes: the emperor, participation in World War II, relations with China and other Asian countries. Recently, references to earthquakes and tsunamis have been perceived in a negative light.

Top brands on mobile market in Japan

device

OS

4.6. Korea

Market size

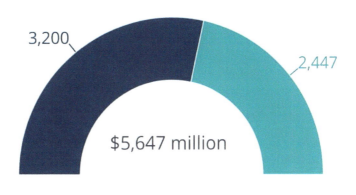

3,200

2,447

$5,647 million

● Mobile games ● PC/console games

Players' spending

Average spending for recreation and culture — $1138

Average spending for games — $195.4

Average spending for mobile games — $118.52

66% use bank cards

85%

of paying gamers spent money on in-game items or virtual goods in the past 6 months

38%

of women and 37% of men bought power-ups

56.27%

average English fluency according to the EF EPI index

39%

of the online population watch video gaming content

Population of South Korea

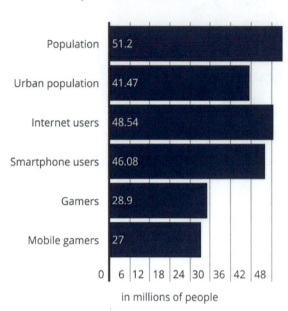

	in millions of people
Population	51.2
Urban population	41.47
Internet users	48.54
Smartphone users	46.08
Gamers	28.9
Mobile gamers	27

Number of gamers in South Korea

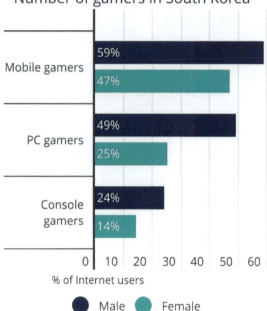

	Male	Female
Mobile gamers	59%	47%
PC gamers	49%	25%
Console gamers	24%	14%

% of Internet users

FACTS ABOUT MOBILE GAMERS

Age and gender distribution

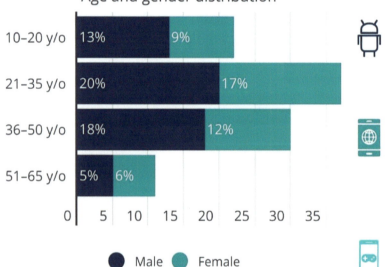

	Male	Female
10–20 y/o	13%	9%
21–35 y/o	20%	17%
36–50 y/o	18%	12%
51–65 y/o	5%	6%

70.59%

of players use Android smartphones and tablets, 29.29% of players use iOS

27.59 GB

of mobile traffic is used in South Korea by a person in average yearly, while the Internet speed is 76.74 Mbit/s

10.4%

the percentage of average consumer spending per capita for recreation and culture made up by mobile games in South Korea

$3.66

is the average user acquisition cost for a mobile game

Top iOS game genres

№	By revenue	By number of downloads
1	Role playng	Action
2	Action	Arcade
3	Strategy	Role playng

Source: Newzoo

48

Korean Culture

Language: Korean.

National symbols: state flag T'aegukki is white with trigrams in the corners and a circular emblem in the center, which symbolizes Yin and Yang. Traditional round symbol framed by five petals and a ribbon with the inscription "Republic of Korea".

Other important cultural elements: traditional Korean attire (hanbok), tiger (mascot of the 1988 and 2018 Olympics), Korean alphabet (Hangeul), fried chicken and beer, food delivery (very accessible and widespread), fascination with celebrities (actors and athletes).

Main holidays (not public holidays are underlined):
New Year (January 1st), Korean New Year (February 4th–6th), March 1st Movement (March 1st), <u>Labor Day (May 1st)</u>, Children's Day (May 5th–6th), Buddha's Birthday (8th day of 4th lunar month), Memorial Day (June 6th), <u>Constitution Day (July 17th)</u>, Liberation Day (August 15th), Harvest Festival (September 12th–14th), National Foundation Day (October 3rd), Hangeul Day (October 9th), Christmas Day (December 25th).

Color associations (traditionally named Obangsaek, but not commonly used now)

North, water	West, metal	East, wood	Center, earth	South, fire

Animal associations

Strength, national animal   Overweight people   Cute

Objectionable content: the number 4 (symbolizes death); poppy flower (associated with drugs); the Japanese flag and any similar images have a negative association.

Objectionable or forbidden themes: Japanese politics, the shape of Korea on the map (because of the uncertain status of some territories), religion.

Top brands on mobile market in South Korea

Culturalization Case
Case: Geopolitics.

 Situation: A game we were working on used some geography that included the Sea of Japan. In Korea, however, it's considered the East Sea.

 Solution: : For the Korean localization, we went with the neutral East Sea, while we left Sea of Japan for the English, Japanese, and Chinese versions.

4.7. India

Market size

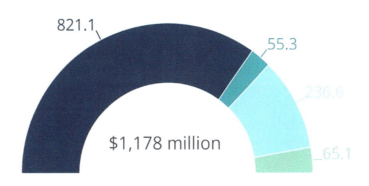

821.1
55.3
236.6
65.1

$1,178 million

● Mobile ● PC/console ● MMO/browser ● Paid subscriptions

Players' spending

Average spending for recreation and culture

Average spending for games

Average spending for mobile games

$11

$4

$4

65.4%
use bank cards

50%
of all gamers own a gaming headset

60%
of people who watch gaming video content watch tips & tricks for games

57.13%
average English fluency according to the EF EPI index

24.11%
of India digital users buy less than one game a month in average, while 42.61% don't buy them at all

Population of India

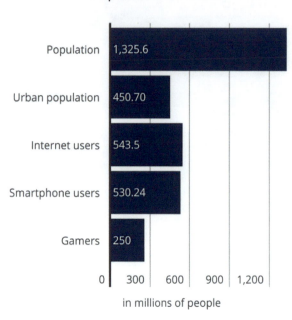

Population	1,325.6
Urban population	450.70
Internet users	543.5
Smartphone users	530.24
Gamers	250

in millions of people

Number of gamers in India

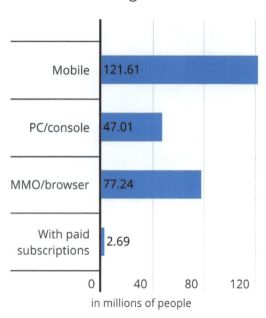

Mobile	121.61
PC/console	47.01
MMO/browser	77.24
With paid subscriptions	2.69

in millions of people

FACTS ABOUT GAMERS

Age and gender distribution

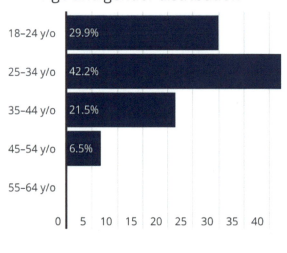

18–24 y/o	29.9%
25–34 y/o	42.2%
35–44 y/o	21.5%
45–54 y/o	6.5%
55–64 y/o	

● 22.4% female, 77.6% male

Popular mobile game genres

№	By revenue	By number of downloads
1	Card games	Board games
2	Strategy	Action
3	Sport	Hyper Casual

Source: Datamagic

87.93%

of players use Android smartphones and tablets, 3.14% — iOS users

150 GB

of mobile traffic is used in India by a person in average yearly, while the Internet speed is 11.02 Mbit/s

42.78%

the percentage of average consumer spending per capita for recreation and culture made up by mobile games in India

$0.05

is the average user acquisition cost for a mobile game

Culture of India

Language: Hindi.

National symbols: flag—Tiranga (Tricolor), emblem—Sarnath Lion Capital, mottos —"Satyameva Jayate" and "Truth Alone Triumphs".

Other important cultural elements: flower— lotus, fruit—mango, tree—banyan, river— Ganges. Yoga has its origins in India and has existed for over 5,000 years. Food—Indian cuisine.

Main holidays (nonregional holidays are <u>underlined</u>): New Year's Day (January 1st), Makar Sankranti/Pongal (January 14th), <u>Public Holiday (january 22nd)</u>, <u>Republic Day (January 26th)</u>, Maha Shivaratri (March 4th), <u>State Holiday for Chief Minister (March 18th)</u>, Holi (March 21-22nd), Ugadi/Gudi Padwa (April 6th), Ram Navami (April 14-15th), Birthday of Rabinrdra Nath Tagore (May 7th) , Buddha Purnima (May 18th), Eid-al-Fitr (June 5th), Bakri Id/Eid al-Adha (August 12th), Independence Day (August 15th), Janmashtami (August 23th, 24th), Ashura (September 9th, 10th), <u>Ananti Chaturdashi (September 12th)</u>, Mahatma Gandhi Jayanti (October 2nd), Diwali (October 27th), Mawlid (November 10th), Christmas (December 25th).

Color associations

Peace, unity and truth	Faith and fertility	Fertility and prosperity	Courage and sacrifice	Lack of desirability, evil, negativity, and inertia

Animal associations

National animal of India	River dolphin—non-human person	Receive prayers in modern-day India	Peafowl—national bird of India

Objectionable content: extreme violence (PUBG was temporarily banned in India).

Objectionable or forbidden themes: beef, mannequins displaying lingerie, pornographic content, alcohol advertisement, homosexuality.

Top brands on mobile market in India

4.8. Indonesia
Market size

570.5

121.5

168.9

6.3

$867.2 million

- ● Mobile
- ● PC/console
- ● MMO/browser
- ● Paid subscriptions

Players' spending

Average spending for recreation and culture	$122
Average spending for games	$9
Average spending for mobile games	$5

34%
use bank cards

96%
of mobile gamers play at home, and 32% of gamers also play at work

65%
of players watch gaming ads to get an in-game bonus

51.58%
low English fluency according to the EF EPI index

53
minutes is the average playing session time for Indonesian gamers

Population of Indonesia

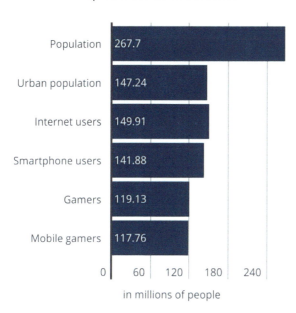

	in millions of people
Population	267.7
Urban population	147.24
Internet users	149.91
Smartphone users	141.88
Gamers	119.13
Mobile gamers	117.76

Number of gamers in Indonesia

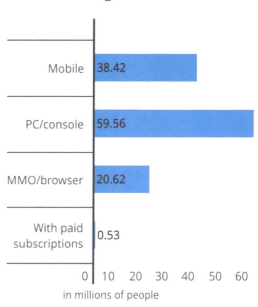

	in millions of people
Mobile	38.42
PC/console	59.56
MMO/browser	20.62
With paid subscriptions	0.53

FACTS ABOUT GAMERS

Age and gender distribution

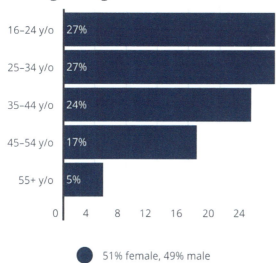

16–24 y/o	27%
25–34 y/o	27%
35–44 y/o	24%
45–54 y/o	17%
55+ y/o	5%

 51% female, 49% male

Popular mobile game genres

№	By revenue	By number of downloads
1	RPG	Action
2	Strategy	RPG
3	Action	Hyper Casual

Source: Datamagic

90.53%

of players use Android smartphones and tablets, 4.64 % of players use iOS

92.56 GB

of mobile traffic is used in Indonesia by a person in average yearly, while the Internet speed is 11.7 Mbit/s

9.56%

the percentage of average consumer spending per capita for recreation and culture made up by mobile games in Indonesia

$0.13

is the average user acquisition cost for a mobile game

Indonesian Culture

Language: Indonesian.

National symbols: red (top) and white (bottom) flag of Indonesia, Garuda Pancasila: Indonesian national emblem is the Garuda with a heraldic shield on its chest and a scroll gripped by its legs.

Other important cultural elements: there are three categories of floral emblems that symbolise Indonesia —the national flower is Melati putih (Jasminum sambac), the flower of charm is Anggrek Bulan (Moon Orchid, Phalaenopsis amabilis), the rare flower is Padma Raksasa Rafflesia (Rafflesia arnoldii).

Main holidays:
Islamic religious holidays: Eid al-Fitr, Eid al-Adha, Isra and Mi'raj, Ashura, Mawlid al-Nabi al-Sharif.
Christian/Catholic religious holidays: Christmas, Easter, Ascension of Jesus.
Buddhist holidays: Waisak Day (Birth of Buddha).
Hindu (Balinese) holidays: Nyepi, Kuningan, Galungan.
Other holidays: Pancasila Day, Independance Day, Chinese New Year.

Color associations

Purity	Active, energy	Brave	Femininity	Sadness, grief

Animal associations

Komodo dragon— national animal

Javan hawk-eagle— national bird

Objectionable content: LGBT related symbols (LGBT are still not openly welcome, so using the symbols can be sensitive), nudity and pornography should be avoided.

Objectionable or forbidden themes: communism symbol (there is a law that prohibit using of this symbol), any kinds of defamation to religious symbols and the flag of the country.

Top on mobile market in Indonesia

4.9. Thailand

Market size+

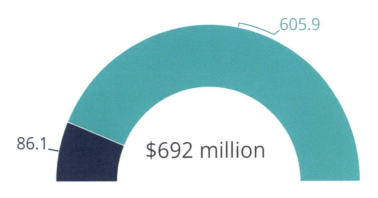

605.9

86.1

$692 million

● Mobile games ● PC and console games

Players' spending

Average spending
for recreation and
culture

$46

30%
use bank cards

Average spending
for mobile games

$1.85

 55%

of gamers spend money in games

 47%

of gamers play every day

 48.54%

very low English fluency according to the EF EPI index

 38

average age of Thailand citizen

Population of Thailand

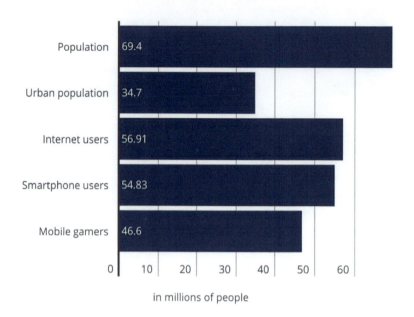

in millions of people

FACTS ABOUT GAMERS

Age and gender distribution

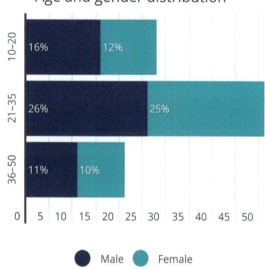

● Male ● Female

Popular mobile game genres

№	By revenue	By number of downloads
1	Shooter	Strategy
2	RPG	Match-3
3	Strategy	RPG

Source: Datamagic

80.49%

of users use Android smartphones and tablets, and 19.08% of players use iOS

66.19 GB

of mobile traffic is used in Thailand by a person in average yearly, while the Internet speed is 19.23 Mbit/s

4.02%

the percentage of average consumer spending per capita for recreation and culture made up by mobile games in Thailand

$0.15

is the average user acquisition cost for a mobile game

Thailand Culture

Language: Thai, Central Thai (historically Siamese).

National symbols: Thai elephant, "Ratchapruek" flower, Thai Pavilion are the official national symbols.

Main holidays (nonpublic and regional holidays are <u>underlined</u>):

New Year's Day (January 1st), <u>Chinese New Year (January–February, depending on the lunar calendar)</u>, Makha Bucha Day (Frbruary or March, depending on the lunar calendar), Chakri Memorial Day (April 6th), Songkran, Thai New Year (April 13th-15th), <u>Easter (April, depending on the lunar calendar)</u>, Labour Day (May 1st), H.M. King's Coronation (May 4th or 6th), Visakha Bucha Day (May), H.M. Queen's Birthday (June 3rd), Asahna Bucha (July), <u>Vegetarian Festival (October, depending on the lunar calendar)</u>, Chulalongkorn Day (October 23nd), <u>Halloween (October 31st)</u>, <u>Loi Krathong (November, depending on the lunar calendar)</u>, Thailand Constitution Day (December 10th), <u>Christmas (December 24th; not as Christ's birthday, more like a gift festival promoted by department stores)</u>.

Color associations

Nation flag: nationalism	Nation flag: monarchy	Nation flag: religion	Homosexual	Military	Sadness	Love, Beautiful

Animal associations

National sport team

Objectionable or forbidden symbols: traditional view would be against using anything relating to Buddha in a disrespectful way. LGBT theme has become more accepted in the last few years, and they openly have boy-love media in bookstores. Nudity in public is considered a bad thing and is against the law. Media features heavy censorship on gore/violence. Drugs, gambling are also against the law. Cigarettes and alcohol are alright.

59

4.10. Malaysia

Market size

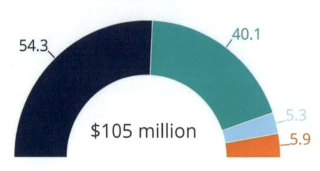

54.3

40.1

5.3

5.9

$105 million

- ● Mobile games
- ● PC/console games
- ● MMO/browser games
- ● Paid subcriptions

Players' spending

Average spending for recreation and culture	$511
Average spending for games	$36
Average spending for mobile games	$13

46%
use bank transfer

 60%

of Malaysian gamers watch video content

 26.42%

of Malaysian players claim that they purchase from 1 to 2 games per month, and 8.09% purchase from 3 to 5 games

 59.32%

high English fluency according to the EF EPI index

 31.09%

of gamers play from 1 to 3 hours per week, while 5.7% play more than 25 hours

Population of Malaysia

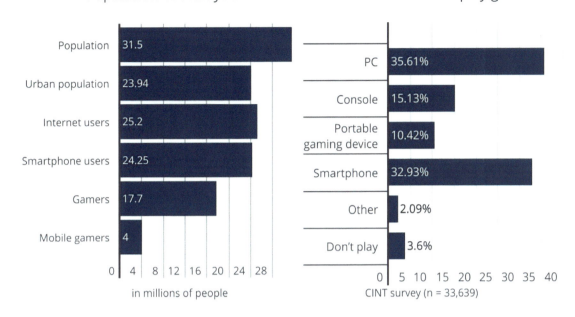

	in millions of people
Population	31.5
Urban population	23.94
Internet users	25.2
Smartphone users	24.25
Gamers	17.7
Mobile gamers	4

Devices used to play games

PC	35.61%
Console	15.13%
Portable gaming device	10.42%
Smartphone	32.93%
Other	2.09%
Don't play	3.6%

CINT survey (n = 33,639)

FACTS ABOUT GAMERS

Age and gender distribution

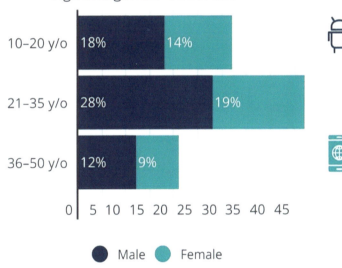

	Male	Female
10–20 y/o	18%	14%
21–35 y/o	28%	19%
36–50 y/o	12%	9%

 Male   Female

Popular mobile game genres

№	By revenue	By number of downloads
1	MOBA	MOBA
2	Shooter	Shooter
3	Sim-life	Battle Royale

Source: Datamagic

78.81%

of players use Android smartphones and tablets, and 19.41% of players use iOS

491.53 GB

people in Malaysia use this amount of mobile traffic in average yearly, while the average Internet speed is 21.26 Mbit/s

2.66%

the percentage of average consumer spending per capita for recreation and culture made up by mobile games in Malaysia

 $0.26

is the average user acquisition cost for a mobile game

Malaysian Culture

Language: Malaysian.

National symbols: coat of arms: adopted in 1965, the Malaysian coat of arms features two tigers supporting a shield (which serves as a representation of the Malaysian states), a crescent and 14-point star at the top. The flag of Malaysia, also known as the Malay: Jalur Gemilang ("Stripes of Glory"), is composed of a field of 14 alternating red and white stripes along the fly and a blue canton bearing a crescent and a 14-point star known as the Bintang Persekutuan (Federal Star). Motto—"Bersekutu Bertambah Mutu" ("Unity Is Strength").

Other important cultural elements: Flower—Chinese hibiscus, Fruit—papaya. Gasing (spinning top) has been a traditional game of the Malays since the ancient times. Roti canai is a popular breakfast and snack dish in Malaysia. Nasi lemak—Malaysian coconut milk rice.

Main holidays:
Ramadan & Eid-al Fitr (one of the most joyful festivals in Malaysia celebrated by Muslims across the country, Eid marks the end of Ramadan, the holy month of abstinence and fasting), Chinese New Year (one of Malaysia's biggest holidays. The date of Chinese New Year is based on the lunar calendar and fluctuates. It always takes places between the end of January and the end of February), Deepavali (also known as Dewali, or the Festival of Lights). It is celebrated in October or November each year. Diwali celebrations can last for about five days.)

Color associations

Most liked color   Most liked color

Animal associations

Overweight   Harimau Malaya (Malaya Tiger) is associated with strength   Most beloved animal

Objectionable content: LGBT is still a taboo concept in Malaysia and should be avoided.

Objectionable or forbidden themes: for the Malay, any referral to pork or pigs is rarely used or should be avoided in Malaysia because of the large Muslim population. For the Hindus, any reference about killing a cow should be avoided.

Top brands on mobile market in Malaysia

4.11. Vietnam

Market size

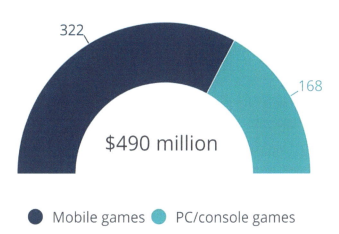

322

168

$490 million

● Mobile games ● PC/console games

Players' spending

Average spending for recreation and culture — $14

Average spending for games — $11

34% use bank cards to pay

Average spending for mobile games — $8.64

 35%

of Vietnamese gamers chat with other players while playing, and 27% of them have dinner when playing

 24.8%

of Vietnamese players claim that they purchase from 1 to 2 games per month, and 10.35% purchase from 3 to 5 games

 53.12%

average English fluency according to the EF EPI index

 31.18%

of gamers play from 1 to 3 hours per week, while 6.18% play more than 25 hours

Population of Vietnam

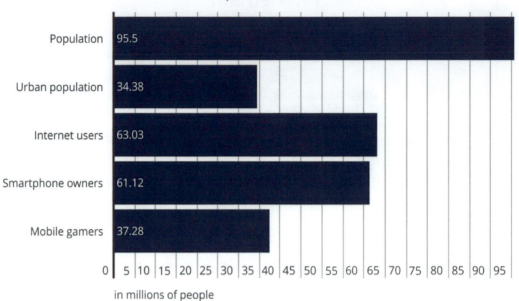

	in millions of people
Population	95.5
Urban population	34.38
Internet users	63.03
Smartphone owners	61.12
Mobile gamers	37.28

FACTS ABOUT GAMERS

Age and gender distribution

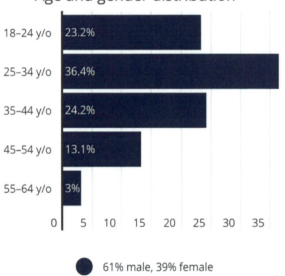

18–24 y/o	23.2%
25–34 y/o	36.4%
35–44 y/o	24.2%
45–54 y/o	13.1%
55–64 y/o	3%

61% male, 39% female

Popular mobile game genres

By revenue	By number of downloads
Strategy	Adventure
RPG	RPG
Action	Hyper Casual

Data provided by DataMagic

55.36%

of players use Android smartphones and tablets, and 40.84% of players use iOS

48.09 GB

of Internet mobile traffic is used in average yearly by a single person in Vietnam, while the Internet speed is 25.3 Mbit/s

61.69%

the percentage of average consumer spending per capita for recreation and culture made up by mobile games in Vietnam

$0.15

is the average user acquisition cost for a mobile game

Vietnamese Culture

Language: Vietnamese.
National symbols: lotus (national flower—symbol of beauty), bamboo (symbol of unity).
Other important cultural elements: ao dai (traditional costume), traditional food pho (noodle soup) and nem (fried spring rolls).

Main holidays:

New Year's Day (January 1st).

Tết (Vietnamese New Year, Vietnamese Lunar New Year, or Tet Holiday), celebrates the arrival of spring based on the Vietnamese calendar. It usually has the date falling in January or February in the Gregorian calendar.

Hùng Kings' Temple Festival is held annually from the 8th to the 11th day of the third lunar month in honor of the Hùng Vương, or Hùng Kings.

Reunification Day (April 30th), Labour Day (May 1st), National Day (September 2nd).

Mid-Autumn Festival (中秋節)—the festival is held on the 15th day of the 8th month of the lunar calendar with a full moon at night, corresponding to mid September to early October of the Gregorian calendar.

Color associations

Innocence, purity	Cool, boss	Lucky (color of new year), dangerous	Nature, cure, medicine	Romantic, sadness	Richness

Animal associations

Strength of old dynasties	Cute	Hardworking	Cute

Objectionable or forbidden themes: any political references and the war against the USA had better be avoided.

Top brands on mobile market in Vietnam

device   OS

4.12. Philippines

Market size

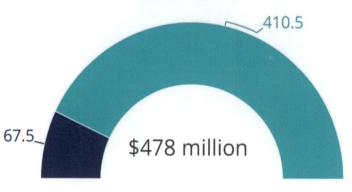

410.5

67.5

$478 million

● Mobile games ● PC & console games

Players' spending

| Average spending for recreation and culture | $42 |
| Average spending for mobile games | $1 |

54%
use bank cards

 54%
of all gamers own a headset

50%
of mobile players are ready to pay for games

67%
of gamers watch video content

 61.84%
high English fluency according to the EF EPI index

Population of Philippines

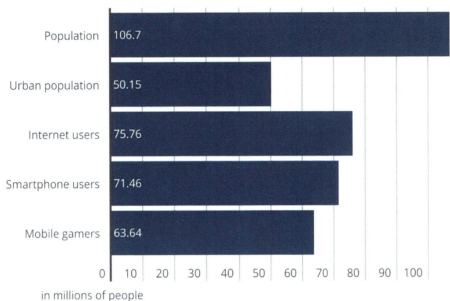

in millions of people

Population	106.7
Urban population	50.15
Internet users	75.76
Smartphone users	71.46
Mobile gamers	63.64

FACTS ABOUT GAMERS

Age and gender distribution

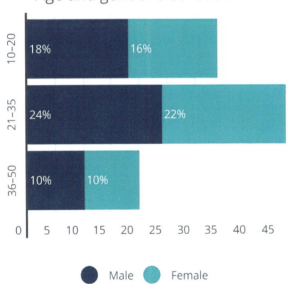

Age	Male	Female
10–20	18%	16%
21–35	24%	22%
36–50	10%	10%

● Male ● Female

77.33%

of players use Android smartphones and tablets, 21.36% of players use iOS

15.1 Mbit/s

is the average Internet speed in Philippines, and $3.16 is the average cost of 1 GB of Internet traffic

67%

of online users watch gaming video content

Popular mobile game genres

№	By revenue	By number of downloads
1	RPG	RPG
2	Shooter	Battle Royale
3	Strategy	Puzzle

$0.15

is the average user acquisition cost for a mobile game

Source: Datamagic

Philippines Culture

Languages: Filipino, English.
National symbols: national flag, national anthem.

Other important cultural elements: Sampaguita, Narra, Philippine eagle, Philippine pearl.

Main holidays:
New Year's Day (January 1st), Chinese New Year (February 5th), People Power Revolution (February 25th), The Day of Valor (April, 9th), Maundy Thursday (April, 18th), Good Friday (April, 19th), Black Saturday (April, 20th), May 01 Labor Day (May, 1st), Public Holiday (May, 13th), Eid'l Fitr (June, 5th), Independence Day (June, 12th), Eidul Adha (August, 12th), Ninoy Aquino Day (August, 21st), National Heroes' Day (Last of August), All Saints' Day (November, 1st), All Souls' Day (November, 2nd), Bonifacio Day (November, 13th), Immaculate Conception Day (December, 8th), Christmas Eve (December, 24th), Christmas Day (December, 25th), Rizal Day (December, 30th), New Year's Eve (December, 31st).

Color associations

Purity, freedom, cleanliness	Death, sadness, darkness	Color of national flag, stars and sun	Death	Sky, ocean, nobility, water
Sadness	Active, energy	Feminity	Skin color, earth	Color of revolution (color of national flag) blood, war, pride and victory, lucky (color of new year), dangerous

Top brands on mobile market in Philippines

device

OS

4.13. USA

Market size+

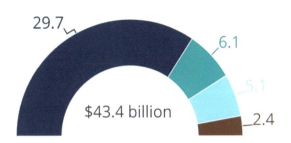

29.7
6.1
5.1
$43.4 billion
2.4

● Digital format sales   ● Physical format sales   ● Hardware

● Accessories & VR

Players' spending

Average spending for recreation and culture	**$3497**
Average spending for games	**$143**
Average spending for mobile games	**$77**

🏧 **71.5%**
use bank cards

 40%

of players' game spending was to give them an advantage, 36%—to level up faster, 25%—to change the look of their character

 56.8%

of players missed sleep to keep playing, and 11.2% missed work to keep playing

 26%

of players use PayPal

 42%

of online population watch gaming video content

Population of the USA

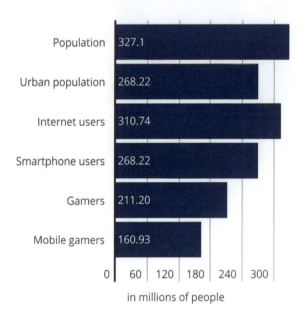

	in millions of people
Population	327.1
Urban population	268.22
Internet users	310.74
Smartphone users	268.22
Gamers	211.20
Mobile gamers	160.93

in millions of people

Number of gamers in the USA

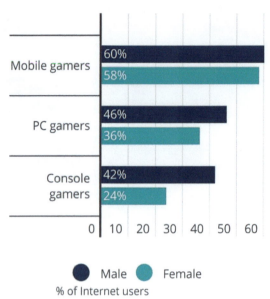

	Male	Female
Mobile gamers	60%	58%
PC gamers	46%	36%
Console gamers	42%	24%

● Male ● Female

% of Internet users

FACTS ABOUT GAMERS

Age and gender distribution

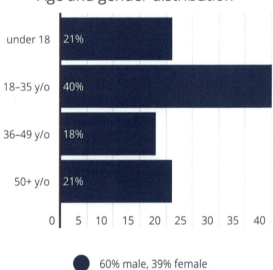

under 18	21%
18–35 y/o	40%
36–49 y/o	18%
50+ y/o	21%

● 60% male, 39% female

Popular mobile game genres

№	By revenue	By number of downloads
1	Match-3	Hyper Casual
2	Party Battlers	Action: Arcade
3	RTS	Action: Scroller

Source: Datamagic

58.33%

of players use iOS smartphones and tablets, 41.23% of players use Android

71.38 GB

of mobile traffic is used in the USA by a person in average yearly, while the Internet speed is 35 Mbit/s

2.22%

the percentage of average consumer spending per capita for recreation and culture made up by mobile games in the USA

$4.71

is the average user acquisition cost for a mobile game

USA Culture

Language: English.

National symbols: flag with stars and stripes; the Great Seal; anthem is "The Star Spangled Banner"; motto is "In God We Trust", the bald eagle.

Other important cultural elements: Statue of Liberty, Liberty Bell, Empire State Building, fast food, McDonald's, American football, highways, large vehicles.

Main holidays (nonpublic and nonfederal holidays are <u>underlined</u>): New Year (January 1st), Martin Luther King Jr. Day (3rd Monday in January), <u>Valentine's Day (February 14th)</u>, President's Day (3rd Monday in February), <u>Mother's Day (2nd Sunday in May)</u>, Memorial Day (last Monday in May), <u>Father's Day (3rd Sunday in May)</u>, Independence Day (July 4th), Labor Day (1st Monday in September), Columbus Day (2nd Monday in October), <u>US Indigenous People's Day (October 12th)</u>, <u>Halloween (October 31st)</u>, Veterans's Day (November 11th), Thanksgiving (4th Thursday in November), Christmas (December 25th).

Color associations

| Purity | Intelligentsia | Anger | Professionalism | Sales | Combination of red, white and blue—patriotism |

Animal associations

| Man's best friend | Cunning | Indecent and deceitful | Symbol of peace |

Objectionable or forbidden symbols (Nazi, swastika, the Holocaust) is not to be used lightly.

Objectionable or forbidden themes (they at buying and selling people or depict black people as the property of white people). It is also best to avoid discrimination.

Top brands on mobile market in the USA

Culturalization Case

Case: Cultural adaptation.

Situation: Russian cultural nuances that American audience wouldn't understand.

Solution: We opted for the closest local equivalents we could find. One example is where we took an achievement name Batsko, that Russian native speakers would associate with the president of Belarus, a country known for its potatoes, with Mr. Potato Head, a character from Toy Story.

4.14. United Kingdom

Market size

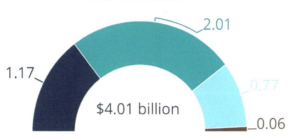

2.01
1.17
0.77
0.06
$4.01 billion

- ● Mobile games
- ● Digital & online games
- ● Physical format sales
- ● Other

Players' spending

Average spending for recreation and culture — **$2472**

Average spending for games — **$143**

Average spending for mobile games — **$91**

78% use bank cards

31%

of male players bought additional content, 24% of female players bought various bonuses

31%

of Internet users watch gaming video content (34% of them watch it on their PCs)

2.7%

of total market size is game-culture spending (toys, merchandising, books, magazines, movies, soundtracks, game events and venues)

6.06%

fraud rate and 0.08% chargeback rate

Population of the UK

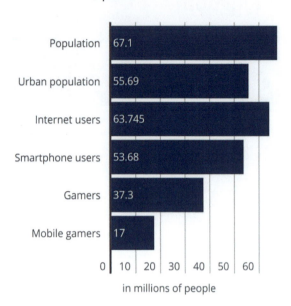

	in millions of people
Population	67.1
Urban population	55.69
Internet users	63.745
Smartphone users	53.68
Gamers	37.3
Mobile gamers	17

Number of gamers in the UK

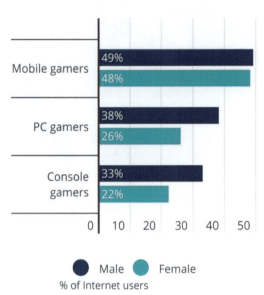

	Male	Female
Mobile gamers	49%	48%
PC gamers	38%	26%
Console gamers	33%	22%

% of Internet users

FACTS ABOUT GAMERS

Age and gender distribution

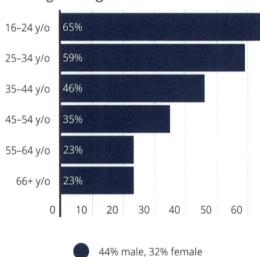

16–24 y/o	65%
25–34 y/o	59%
35–44 y/o	46%
45–54 y/o	35%
55–64 y/o	23%
66+ y/o	23%

● 44% male, 32% female

Popular mobile game genres

№	By revenue	By number of downloads
1	Match-3	Action: Arcade
2	RTS	Hyper Casual
3	Crafting & Building	RTS

Source: Datamagic

56.44%

of players use iOS smartphones and tablets, 42.06% of players use Android

73.87 GB

of mobile traffic is used in the UK by a person in average yearly, while the Internet speed is 30.93 Mbit/s

3.69%

the percentage of average consumer spending per capita for recreation and culture made up by mobile games in the UK

$4.25

is the average user acquisition cost for a mobile game

UK Culture

Language: English 98% (official), Scots 2%, Welsh 1%, Ulster Scots, Scottish Gaelic, Irish <0.1%.

Flags:
The UK—Union Jack, England—St. George's Cross, Scotland—St. Andrew's Cross, N. Ireland—St. Patrick's Cross, Wales—Red Dragon, Green Field.

National flowers:
England—red rose (Tudor Rose), Scotland—thistle, N. Ireland—shamrock (three-leaf clover), Wales—daffodil.

National sports:
football, rugby, cricket.

Cultural symbols:
The UK/England: tea, fish and chips, beer, pubs, Sunday roast, Yorkshire pudding, humor.
Scotland: kilts, haggis, Scotch whiskey.
Wales: sheep.

London: Big Ben, London Eye, red bus, red telephone box, black cabs, underground.

Main holidays (public holidays are <u>underlined</u>):
<u>New Year's Day (January 1st)</u>, Robert Burns Night (January 25th), St. Valentine's Day (February 14th), Shrove Tuesday (Before Ash Wednesday), St. Patrick's Day (March 17th), April Fools' Day (April 1st), <u>Easter celebration (April 19th & 20th)</u>, St. George's Day (April 23rd), Father's Day (June 16th), Halloween (October 31st), Guy Fawkes, or Fireworks Night (November 5th), <u>Christmas Day (December 25th)</u>, <u>Boxing Day (December 26th)</u>, New Year's Eve (December 31st).

Color associations

Innocence	Death, mourning	Anger, love, fire, danger	Hope or envy	Loyalty, cold	Envy, guile

Animal associations

Industrious	Wise	Weakness	Dumb	Noble and important	Motherhood	Evil in British folklore	Unclean

Objectionable content: media that contains flashing imagery (epilepsy), strong violence, gore, killing, guns (weapons), drugs, adult language (swearing), nudity & scenes of sexual nature usually must have a warning label and be age rated appropriately.

Forbidden subjects: Britain is a multicultural/ethnically diverse country. Racial discrimination is an offence.

Top on mobile market in the UK

4.15. Canada

Market size

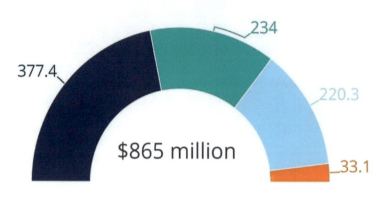

$865 million

- 377.4
- 234
- 220.3
- 33.1

● Mobile ● PC/console ● MMO/browser ● Paid subscriptions

Players' spending

Average spending for recreation and culture	$2058
Average spending for games	$100
Average spending for mobile games	$29

62%
use bank cards

21.95%

of players spend from 4 to 10 hours a week playing video/computer games, 5.51% of players spend more than 25 hours a week

40.5%

of players stated that they usually play games whenever they are bored

66%

of paying gamers spent money on in-game items

31%

of the online population watches gaming video content

Population of Canada

	in millions of people
Population	37.1
Urban population	30.05
Internet users	33.76
Smartphone users	34.87
Gamers	23
Mobile gamers	12.6

0 6 12 18 24 30 36

in millions of people

Number of gamers in Canada

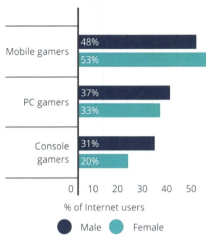

	Male	Female
Mobile gamers	48%	53%
PC gamers	37%	33%
Console gamers	31%	20%

0 10 20 30 40 50

% of Internet users

● Male ● Female

FACTS ABOUT GAMERS

Average age and gender distribution (2009–2018)

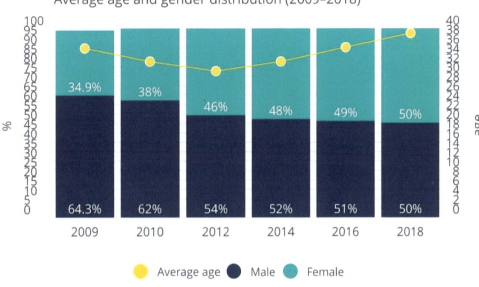

	2009	2010	2012	2014	2016	2018
Female	34.9%	38%	46%	48%	49%	50%
Male	64.3%	62%	54%	52%	51%	50%

● Average age ● Male ● Female

60.14%

of players use Android smartphones and tablets, and 38.79% of players use iOS

1.46%

the percentage of average consumer spending per capita for recreation and culture made up by mobile games in Canada

56.66 GB

of mobile traffic is used in Canada by a person in average yearly, while the Internet speed is 63.81 Mbit/s

$5.12

is the average user acquisition cost for a mobile game

Popular mobile game genres

№	By revenue	By number of downloads
1	Puzzle: Match-3	Action
2	Action	Hyper Casual
3	Action: Battle Royale	Puzzle (excl. Match-3)

Source: Datamagic

Canadian Culture

Language: English, French.
National symbols: maple leaf. Other prominent symbols include the sports of hockey and lacrosse, the beaver, the Royal Canadian Mounted Police, the Canadian Rockies, and more recently the totem pole and Inuksuk.

Other important cultural elements: Canadian beer, maple syrup, tuques, canoes, nanaimo bars, butter tarts and the Quebec dish of poutine being defined as uniquely Canadian.

Main holidays (regional and nonpublic holidays are <u>underlined</u>): New Year (January 1st), <u>Family Day (February 17th)</u>, Easter (April, depends on the lunar calendar), <u>Mother's Day (May 10th)</u>, Vicroria Day (May 18th), <u>Father's Day (June 21st)</u>, Canada Day (July 1st), Labour Day (1st Monday in September), <u>Thanksgiving (2nd Monday in October)</u>, <u>Remembrance Day (November 11th)</u>, Christmas (December 25th), <u>Boxing Day (December 26th)</u>.

Color associations

Love

Environment / environmentalism

Royalty

Purity

Death, mourning

Animal associations

Beaver—national symbol

Canadian horse— national symbol

Objectionable content: swastika images; symbols and images of extremist organizations; take care when using any religious symbol.

Objectionable or forbidden themes: better to avoid imagery with alcohol and tobacco products, as well as depicting violent scenes in products meant for children.

Top brands on mobile market in Canada

4.16. Germany

Market Size

1.5

1.78

0.78

$4.06 billion

in billions of US dollars

● Mobile games ● Console games ● PC games

Players' spending

Average spending for recreation and culture

$2108

Average spending for games

$119

Average spending for mobile games

$95

26%
use e-wallets to pay

26%

of men bought DLC/expansion packs, 20% of women bought power-ups

29%

of all players will be 45 or older in 2019; the average age is 36.4

63.74%

very high English fluency according to the EF EPI index

5%

fraud rate and 0.08% chargeback rate

Population of Germany

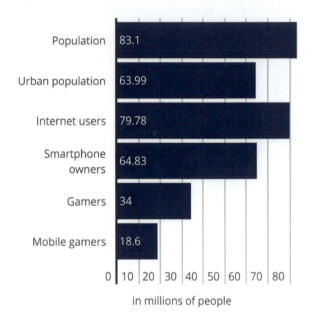

	in millions of people
Population	83.1
Urban population	63.99
Internet users	79.78
Smartphone owners	64.83
Gamers	34
Mobile gamers	18.6

Number of gamers in Germany

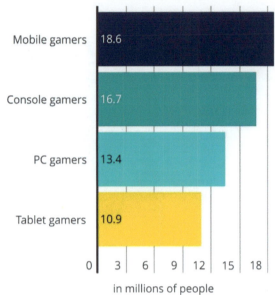

	in millions of people
Mobile gamers	18.6
Console gamers	16.7
PC gamers	13.4
Tablet gamers	10.9

FACTS ABOUT GAMERS

Age and gender distribution

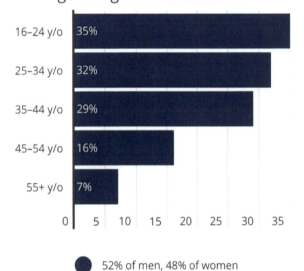

16–24 y/o	35%
25–34 y/o	32%
35–44 y/o	29%
45–54 y/o	16%
55+ y/o	7%

● 52% of men, 48% of women

Popular mobile game genres

By revenue	By number of downloads
Match-3	Hyper Casual
Party Battlers	Action: Arcade
MMO Strategy	Puzzles (excl. Match-3)

data provided by DataMagic

63.61%

of players use Android smartphones and tablets, and 35.17% of players use iOS

94.89 GB

of mobile traffic is used in Germany by a person in average yearly, while the average Internet speed is 31.9 Mbit/s

4.54%

the percentage of average consumer spending per capita for recreation and culture made up by mobile games in Germany

$4.08

is the average user acquisition cost for a mobile game

German Culture

Language: German.

National symbols: heraldic eagle, black, red, and yellow flag, national anthem.

Other important cultural elements: beer, sausages, pretzels, German shepherds, the waltz, Till Eulenspiegel, Oktoberfest.

Main holidays (nonreligious holidays are <u>underlined</u>):
<u>New Year (January 1st)</u>, the Friday before Easter and the Monday after it (depends on the lunar calendar), <u>Labor Day (May 1st)</u>, Ascension Day (the 39th day after Easter), Pentecost (the 7th Monday after Easter), <u>Unity Day (October 3rd)</u>, Christmas (December 25th), St. Stephen's Day (December 26th).

Color associations

Innocence	Death	Anger, love, fire, danger	Hope or envy	Loyalty or coldness	Envy or cowardness

Animal associations

Industrious	Wise	Weakness	Dumb	Conceited	Motherhood	Doom	Unclean

Objectionable or forbidden symbols: any symbol of Nazi Germany. In 2018 German law was amended to allow the display of unconstitutional images in games as works of art, but every instance is reviewed by a committee on an individual basis. The evaluation criteria are still being developed.

Objectionable or forbidden themes: Nazism; depicting killing of human beings in products intended for people under the age of 18 is also illegal.

Top brands on mobile market in Germany

Culturalization Case

Case: History, past and present.

 Situation: A game set in ancient Rome had a line where the character put on a lemur costume that came with the figure of a skeleton. In ancient Rome, restless souls were called lemurs, though the association these days is just with the cute little animals themselves.

 Solution: We decided to just have the character put on a skeleton costume.

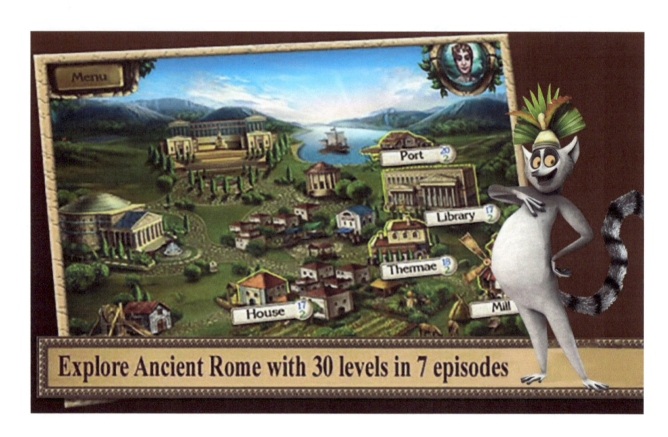

4.17. France

Market size

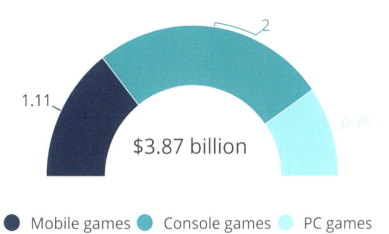

2

1.11

0.75

$3.87 billion

● Mobile games ● Console games ● PC games

Players' spending

Average spending for recreation and culture
$1697

Average spending for games
$118

Average spending for mobile games
$67

53.9% use bank cards

 31%
of male players and 20% of female players bought additional content for games

 29%
of Internet users watch gaming video content (47% of them watch it on their PCs)

 55.49%
average English fluency according to the EF EPI index

 2.88%
fraud rate and 0.06% chargeback rate

Population of France

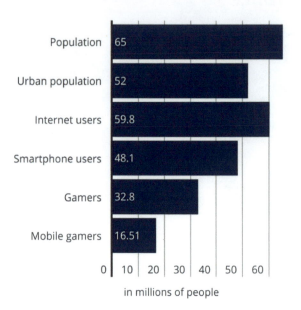

Population	65
Urban population	52
Internet users	59.8
Smartphone users	48.1
Gamers	32.8
Mobile gamers	16.51

in millions of people

Number of gamers in France

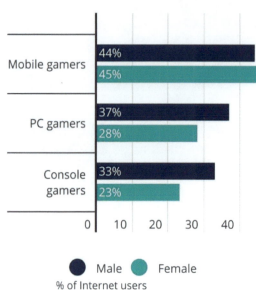

	Male	Female
Mobile gamers	44%	45%
PC gamers	37%	28%
Console gamers	33%	23%

● Male ● Female

% of Internet users

FACTS ABOUT GAMERS

Age distribution

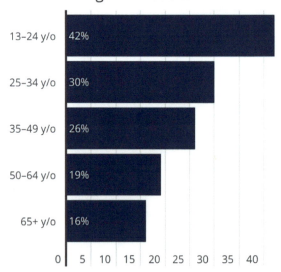

13–24 y/o	42%
25–34 y/o	30%
35–49 y/o	26%
50–64 y/o	19%
65+ y/o	16%

Popular mobile game genres

№	By revenue	By number of downloads
1	Turn-based RPG (Party Battlers)	Action: Arcade
2	Action: Arcade	Hyper Casual
3	RTS	Puzzles (excl. Match-3)

Source: Datamagic

61.14%

of players use Android smartphones and tablets, and 37.64% of players use iOS

176.59 GB

people in France use this amount of mobile traffic in average yearly, while the average Internet speed is 45.83 Mbit/s

3.98%

the percentage of average consumer spending per capita for recreation and culture made up by mobile games in France

$0.55

is the average user acquisition cost for a mobile game

French Culture

Language: French.

National symbols: blue, white, and red flag; anthem is "La Marseillaise", the motto is "Liberty, Equality, Fraternity".

Other important cultural elements: Eiffel Tower, Gallic rooster, delicacies (especially baguettes, cheese and wine), style and fashion (the stereotypical image of a Frenchman in a sailor's uniform and beret may be perceived negatively).

 Main holidays (nonpublic holidays are <u>underlined</u>):
New Year (January 1st), <u>Valentine's Day (February 14th)</u>, Easter (first Sunday after April 21th), Labour Day (May 1st), V-E Day (May 8th), Ascension Day (40th day of Easter), Whit Monday (7th Monday after Easter), <u>Mother's Day (last Sunday in May)</u>, <u>Father's Day (third Sunday in June)</u>, Bastille Day (June 14th), Assumption of Mary (August 15th), <u>Halloween (October 31st)</u>, All Saints' Day (November 1st), Armistice Day (November 11th), Christmas (December 25th).

Color associations

| Bridal | Happiness, tenderness, female color | Anger | Football | Envy |

Animal associations

| Filth | Cleverness | Stupidity | Slowness | Pride | Strength |

Objectionable content: religious symbols, images of the swastika, emblems of terrorist organizations.

Objectionable or forbidden themes: discrimination of any kind is prohibited by law, including sexism, racism, homophobia, transphobia, antisemitism, etc. Mention of recent wars (in Indochina and Algeria) in which France participated is undesirable. The First and Second World Wars are perceived as less painful.

Top brands on mobile market in France

device   OS

4.18. Russia

Market size

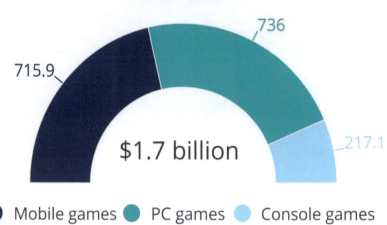

715.9   736   217.1

$1.7 billion

● Mobile games   ● PC games   ● Console games

Players' spending

Average spending for recreation and culture	$492
Average spending for games	$26
Average spending for mobile games	$27

88.9%

use bank cards to pay

81%

of paying gamers spent money on in-game items or virtual goods in the past 6 months

42%

of women and 36% of men bought power-ups

52.96%

average English fluency according to the EF EPI index

0.75%

fraud rate and 0.82% chargeback rate

Population of Russia

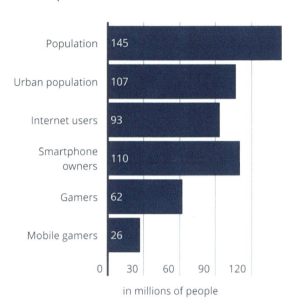

	in millions of people
Population	145
Urban population	107
Internet users	93
Smartphone owners	110
Gamers	62
Mobile gamers	26

Number of gamers in Russia

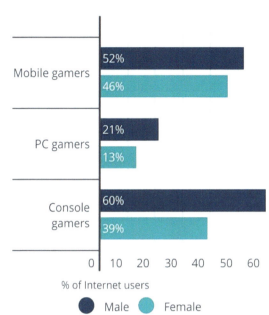

% of Internet users

● Male   ● Female

	Male	Female
Mobile gamers	52%	46%
PC gamers	21%	13%
Console gamers	60%	39%

FACTS ABOUT MOBILE GAMERS

Smartphone owners age distribution

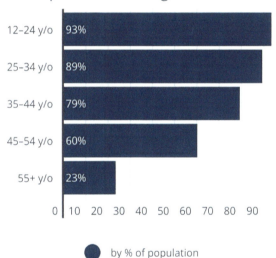

	by % of population
12–24 y/o	93%
25–34 y/o	89%
35–44 y/o	79%
45–54 y/o	60%
55+ y/o	23%

● by % of population

Popular mobile game genres

№	By LTV
1	MMO Strategy
2	Match-3
3	Action: shooter

Source: Datamagic

67.83%

of players use Android smartphones and tablets, and 30.25 % of players use iOS

240.66 GB

people in Russia use this amount of mobile traffic in average yearly, while the Internet speed is 20.12 Mbit/s

5.58%

the percentage of average consumer spending per capita for recreation and culture made up by mobile games in Russia

$2.17

is the average user acquisition cost for a mobile game

Russian culture

Language: Russian.

National symbols: tricolor, double-headed eagle, outline of the Kremlin, St. Basil's Cathedral, Saint George the Victorious (coat of arms of Moscow), pancakes, vodka, Matryoshka doll, balalaika.

Other important cultural elements: hammer and sickle, red flag (communist), USSR, Pyotr Tchaikovsky, Leo Tolstoy, Kalashnikov rifle, sputnik, bears, russian trapper hat.

 Main holidays:
New Year (January 1st–8th), Defence of the Fatherland Day (formerly Red Army Day, February 23rd), International Women's Day (March 8th), Day of Spring and Labor (formerly International Workers' Day (May 1st), Victory Day (May 9th), Russia Day (June 12th), Day of Unity (November 4th).

Color associations

Sky; gay men are called "blue"	Grief, sorrow, mourning	Purity, innocence	Excrement	Sun	Feminity

Animal associations

Favorite animal of the Russian Internet	Friend, loyalty	Dirty	Sly, cunning	Stubborn	Annoying, bad person (about a man)

Objectionable or forbidden themes: promotion of homosexuality among minors, symbols of outlawed organizations (ISIS, etc.), presenting military conflicts from the point of view which is different from the official one (Syria, etc.), offending the feelings of believers (Orthodox and Muslims).

Top brands on mobile market in Russia

device

Culturalization Case

Case: Depictions of homosexuality[43].

 Situation: A European developer came out with a game rated 3+ that had a homosexual plot line.

 Solution: When it came time to localize for Russia, we made sure the homosexual relationship stayed limited to friendship. Otherwise, the game would have earned itself an 18+ rating that would have cut out a large part of the target audience.

---

43 Illustration from Pride Run Game

4.19. Italy

Market size

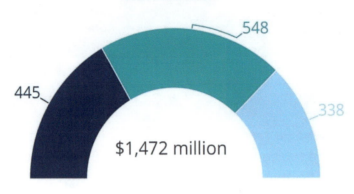

548

445

338

$1,472 million

● Mobile games ● Digital (PC/consoles) ● Physical (PC/consoles)

Players' spending

Average spending for recreation and culture	$1382
Average spending for games	$59
Average spending for mobile games	$37

33.8%
use bank cards

42%

of players receive information about video games from friends and family, 23%—from social media, and 15%—from gaming websites

37%

of console players use PlayStation, and 20% of PC players use Steam

55.77%

average English fluency according to the EF EPI index

0.5%

fraud rate and 0.06% chargeback rate

Population of Italy

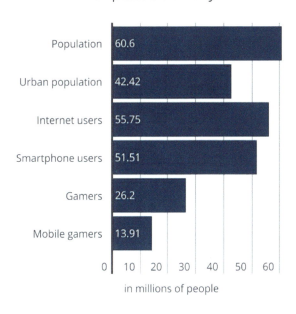

	in millions of people
Population	60.6
Urban population	42.42
Internet users	55.75
Smartphone users	51.51
Gamers	26.2
Mobile gamers	13.91

Number of gamers in Italy

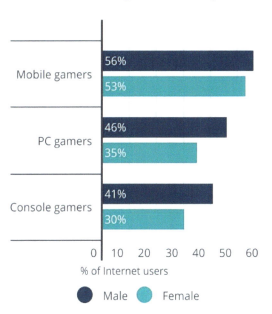

% of Internet users

	Male	Female
Mobile gamers	56%	53%
PC gamers	46%	35%
Console gamers	41%	30%

● Male ● Female

FACTS ABOUT GAMERS

Age and gender distribution

	6-10 y/o	11-14 y/o	15-24 y/o	25-34 y/o	35-44 y/o	45-64 y/o
female	5%	4%	11%	9%	7%	9%
male	5%	5%	13%	10%	8%	13%

○ 54% male ● 46% female

Popular mobile game genres

№	By revenue	By number of downloads
1	Puzzle: Match-3	Action: Arcade
2	Strategy: RTS	Hyper Casual
3	Battler	Action

Source: Datamagic

69.95%

of players use Android smartphones and tablets, 28.34% — iOS users

266.47 GB

of mobile traffic is used in Italy by a person in average yearly, while the Internet speed is 32.93 Mbit/s

2.73%

the percentage of average consumer spending per capita for recreation and culture made up by mobile games in Italy

 $0.26

is the average user acquisition cost for a mobile game

Italian Culture

Language: Italian.

National symbols: green, white and red flag; coat of arms with a five-pointed star, as well as oak and olive branches; anthem is "Song of the Italians".

Other important cultural elements: pasta, pizza, ancient Roman heritage, architecture, painting, fashion.

 **Main holidays (nonreligious holidays are <u>underlined</u>):**
<u>New Year (January 1st)</u>, Epiphany (January 6th), Easter (depends on the lunar calendar), <u>Liberation Day (April 25th)</u>, <u>Labour Day (May 1st)</u>, <u>Republic Day (June 2nd)</u>, Assumption of Mary (August 15th), All Saints' Day (November 1st), Immaculate Conception (December 8th), Christmas (December 25th), St. Stephen's Day (December 26th).

Color associations

Innocence and purity

Health, freshness

Animal associations

Filth

Smart person

Cowardice

Braveness and strength

Unpleasant person

Objectionable content: swastika images; symbols and images of extremist organizations; take care when using any religious symbol.

Objectionable or forbidden themes: better to avoid imagery with alcohol and tobacco products, as well as depicting violent scenes in products meant for children.

Top brands on mobile market in Italy

4.20. Spain

Market size

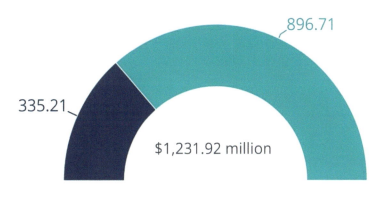

896.71

335.21

$1,231.92 million

● Mobile games ● PC/console games

Players' spending

Average spending for recreation and culture — $1273

Average spending for games — $73

Average spending for mobile games — $36

43.2%

use bank cards

62%

of paying gamers spent money on in-game items

43%

of Internet users watch gaming video content (48% of them watch it on their PCs)

55.85%

average English fluency according to the EF EPI index

1.29%

fraud rate and 0.06% chargeback rate

Population of Spain

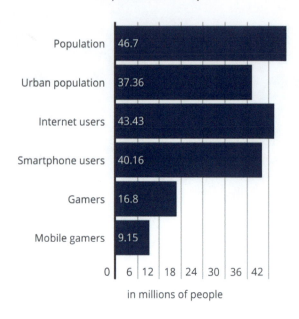

Population	46.7
Urban population	37.36
Internet users	43.43
Smartphone users	40.16
Gamers	16.8
Mobile gamers	9.15

0 6 12 18 24 30 36 42

in millions of people

Number of gamers in Spain

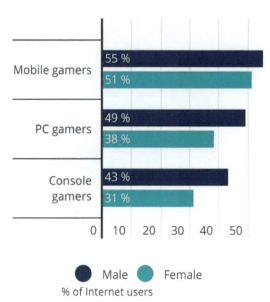

	Male	Female
Mobile gamers	55 %	51 %
PC gamers	49 %	38 %
Console gamers	43 %	31 %

0 10 20 30 40 50

● Male   ● Female

% of Internet users

FACTS ABOUT GAMERS

Age and gender distribution

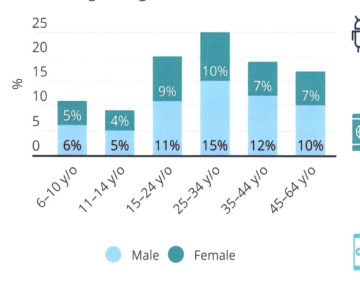

	6–10 y/o	11–14 y/o	15–24 y/o	25–34 y/o	35–44 y/o	45–64 y/o
Female	5%	4%	9%	10%	7%	7%
Male	6%	5%	11%	15%	12%	10%

● Male   ● Female

76.73%

of players use Android smartphones and tablets, 15.38% of players use iOS

119 GB

of mobile traffic is used in Spain by a person in average yearly, while the Internet speed is 33.7 Mbit/s

2.88%

the percentage of average consumer spending per capita for recreation and culture made up by mobile games in Spain

$0.63

is the average user acquisition cost for a mobile game

Popular mobile games genres

№	By revenue	By number of downloads
1	Strategy	Action
2	Match-3	Hyper Casual
3	Battler	Puzzles (excl. Match-3)

Source: Datamagic

Spanish Culture

Language: Spanish.

National symbols: state yellow and red flag and provincial flags; coat of arms with the image of the Pillars of Hercules; anthem is "La Marcha Real"; motto is "Plus ultra".

Other important cultural elements: paella, wine, Spanish guitar, traditional dances, football fans, large families, bullfighting.

Main holidays (nonreligious holidays are <u>underlined</u>):
<u>New Year (January 1st)</u>, Epiphany (January 6th), Easter (Apil, depends on the lunar calendar), <u>Labour Day (May 1st)</u>, Assumption of Mary (August 15th), <u>National Day of Spain (October 12th)</u>, All Saints' Day (November 1st), Immaculate Conception (December 8th), Christmas (December 25th).

Color associations

Bridal

Mourning

Passion

Animal associations

Filth

Fastness

Stupidity

Insanity

Strength

Objectionable content: Nazi symbols and emblems, religious and political symbols. It is also best to avoid showing alcohol and tobacco products to persons under 18.

Objectionable or forbidden themes: conducting bullfights (the expediency of this has been a topic of heated discussion), mention of the royal family in a negative context.

Top on mobile market in Spain

device

OS

4.21. Brazil

Market size

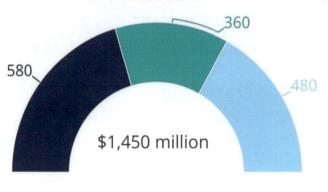

580 360 480

$1,450 million

● Mobile games ● PC games ● Console games

Players' spending

Average spending for recreation and culture	$61
Average spending for games	$19
Average spending for mobile games	$10

59% use bank cards

 38%

of male players and 35% of female players bought additional content

 59%

of Internet users watch gaming video content (35% of them watch it on their PC)

 50.93%

low English fluency according to the EF EPI index

 59.2%

of developers developed products for mobile devices in 2018, while 9.9% of developers created games for standalone computer users

Population of Brazil

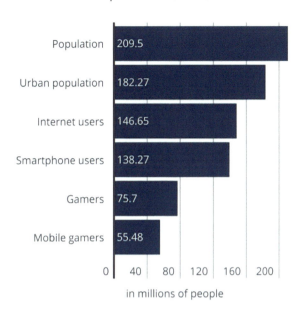

	in millions of people
Population	209.5
Urban population	182.27
Internet users	146.65
Smartphone users	138.27
Gamers	75.7
Mobile gamers	55.48

Number of gamers in Brazil

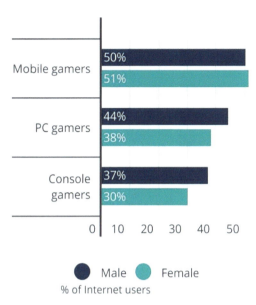

	Male	Female
Mobile gamers	50%	51%
PC gamers	44%	38%
Console gamers	37%	30%

● Male   ● Female

% of Internet users

FACTS ABOUT GAMERS

Age and gender distribution

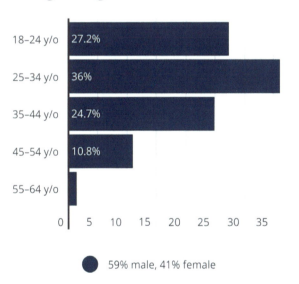

18–24 y/o	27.2%
25–34 y/o	36%
35–44 y/o	24.7%
45–54 y/o	10.8%
55–64 y/o	

● 59% male, 41% female

Popular mobile game genres

№	By revenue	By number of downloads
1	Action	Action
2	RTS	Hyper Casual
3	Match-3	Shooter (FPS)

Source: Datamagic

83.67%

of players use Android smartphones and tablets, and 13.27% of players use iOS

118.29 GB

of mobile traffic is used in Brazil by a person in average yearly, while the average Internet speed is 21.39 Mbit/s

17.14%

the percentage of average consumer spending per capita for recreation and culture made up by mobile games in Brazil

$1.42

is the average user acquisition cost for a mobile game

Brazilian Culture

Language: Brazilian Portuguese.

National symbols: green flag with a horizontal yellow rhombus and a dark blue circle depicting nine constellations; coat of arms with a five-pointed star, framed by branches of the coffee tree and flowering tobacco; anthem is "Hino Nacional Brasileir motto is "Order and Progress".

Other important cultural elements: Christ the Redeemer statue, football (the team, a source of national pride, has a yellow-green uniform), Carnival, great holidays.

Main holidays:
Christmas (December 25th), New Year (January 1st), Valentine's Day (February 14th), Carnival (40 days before Easter), Easter (depends on the lunar calendar), Independence Day (September 7th), Feast Day of Our Lady Aparecida (October 12th).

Color associations

Peace	Sorrow	Passion	Hope	Romance	Money

Animal associations

Symbols of nation	Antagonists in kids fairy tales	According to legends, kidnap children	Dumb	Drunkard

Objectionable content: emblems of extremist organizations, Nazi symbols. Imagery of alcohol and tobacco products are permitted, except for those scenes where they are being consumed by minors.

Forbidden themes: Brazilians regard everything with humor, except subjects of national pride. Therefore, it's best not to joke about religion, politics or football.

Top brands on mobile market in Brazil

Culturalization Case

Case: Intra-country cultural differences.

 Situation: A trading card game rated PEGI 7. Two editors were hard at work. One of them noticed that the word "girl" was translated as "rapariga," saying that we needed to avoid that—it's a derogatory word that can mean something like "slut" in the northern regions of Brazil.

 Solution: Replace the word "rapariga" with "mulher."

4.22. Mexico

Market size

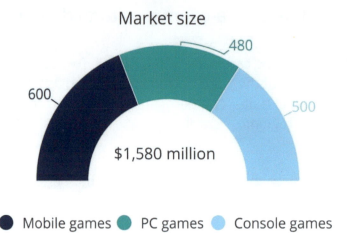

600
480
500

$1,580 million

● Mobile games ● PC games ● Console games

Players' spending

Average spending for recreation and culture	$355	
Average spending for games	$28	
Average spending for mobile games	$17	

45%
use bank cards

54%

of the online population watch gaming video content

30.34%

of Mexican players claim that they purchase from 1 to 2 games per month, and 9.72% purchase from 3 to 5 games

49.76%

low English fluency according to the EF EPI index

30.97%

of gamers play from 1 to 3 hours per week, while 2.64% play more than 25 hours per week

Population of Mexico

	in millions of people
Population	126.2
Urban population	100.96
Internet users	84.55
Smartphone users	78.24
Gamers	55.8
Mobile gamers	34.38

Number of gamers in Mexico

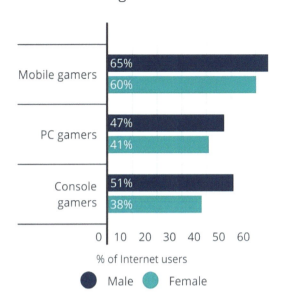

	Male	Female
Mobile gamers	65%	60%
PC gamers	47%	41%
Console gamers	51%	38%

% of Internet users

● Male   ● Female

FACTS ABOUT GAMERS

Age and gender distribution

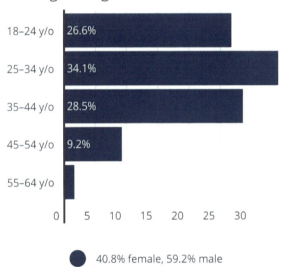

18–24 y/o	26.6%
25–34 y/o	34.1%
35–44 y/o	28.5%
45–54 y/o	9.2%
55–64 y/o	

● 40.8% female, 59.2% male

Popular mobile game genres

№	By revenue	By number of downloads
1	Shooter	Hyper Casual
2	RTS	Shooter
3	Battler	Runner

Source: Datamagic

78.48%

of players use Android smartphones and tablets, and 20.12% of players use iOS

25.47 GB

people in Mexico use this amount of mobile traffic in average yearly, while the average Internet speed is 23.78 Mbit/s

4.92%

the percentage of average consumer spending per capita for recreation and culture made up by mobile games in Mexico

$0.11

is the average user acquisition cost for a mobile game

Mexican Culture

Language: Mexican Spanish.

National symbols: the most important would be the Mexican coat of arms: you can find it on cars and obviously on all government buildings.

Other important cultural elements: the poinsettia, a native plant from Mexico, has been associated with Christmas carrying the Christian symbolism of the Star of Bethlehem. Clay pottery, embroidered cotton garments, wool shawls and outer garments with angular designs, colorful baskets and rugs are some of the common items associated with Mexican folk art.

Main holidays (not an official holidays are <u>underlined</u>):
New Year's Day (January 1st), Constitution Day (First Monday in February), Benito Juarez's Birthday (3rd Monday in March), Easter celebration (April 18th & 19th), Labor day (May 1st), <u>Mother's Day (May 10th)</u>, <u>Father's Day (3rd Sunday in June)</u>, Independence Day (September 16th), <u>Mexico Day of the Races (October 12th)</u>, <u>Day of the Dead (November 2nd)</u>, Revolution Day (3rd Monday of November), Virgin of Guadalupe Day (December 12th), Christmas Day (December 25th).

Color associations

Luck, money, energy (sun), happiness	Love, passion, blood, anger, fire, war, devil	Nature, environment, youth (inexpert people), fertility.	military, patriotism	Innocence, purity, neatness, peace, fraternity	Mourning, death, seriousness, formality

Animal associations

Most popular pet animal

In some rural areas cats are considered servants to the devil

Objectionable content: Mexican society is very religious/conservative, therefore, homosexuality/LGBT is not well seen. Additionally, it is also a very Latin culture, so it is male dominated, and sometimes chauvinism is evident in people's behavior.

Objectionable or forbidden themes: much of Mexico is Catholic, and controversial topics surrounding religious debates are best kept for private conversation among close friends or not discussed at all.

Top on mobile market in Mexico

4.23. Turkey

Market size

400

453

$853 million

in millions of US dollars

● Mobile games ● PC + console games

Players' spending

Average spending for recreation and culture — $427

Average spending for games — $28

Average spending for mobile games — $36

64%

use bank cards to pay

 72%

of Internet users play games on mobile devices

 42%

of men and 30% of women make online transactions

 36%

play games streamed live via the Internet, and 27% watch live streams in Turkey

 52.96%

average English fluency according to the EF EPI index

Population of Turkey

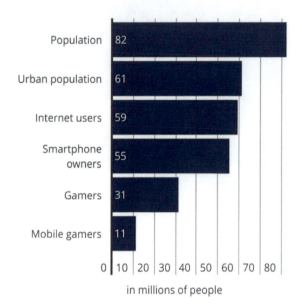

	in millions of people
Population	82
Urban population	61
Internet users	59
Smartphone owners	55
Gamers	31
Mobile gamers	11

in millions of people

Most active social media platforms

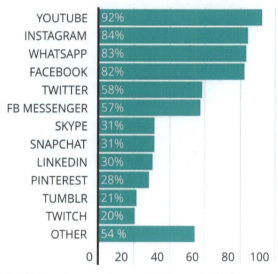

YOUTUBE	92%
INSTAGRAM	84%
WHATSAPP	83%
FACEBOOK	82%
TWITTER	58%
FB MESSENGER	57%
SKYPE	31%
SNAPCHAT	31%
LINKEDIN	30%
PINTEREST	28%
TUMBLR	21%
TWITCH	20%
OTHER	54 %

% of Internet users who report using each platform (survey based), Globalwebindex (Q2 & Q3 2018)

FACTS ABOUT INTERNET USERS

Social media audience profile

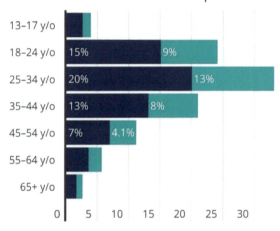

	Male	Female
13–17 y/o		
18–24 y/o	15%	9%
25–34 y/o	20%	13%
35–44 y/o	13%	8%
45–54 y/o	7%	4.1%
55–64 y/o		
65+ y/o		

● Male ● Female

Based on the combined advertising audiences of Facebook, Instagram and Facebook Messenger

Popular mobile game genres

№	By revenue	By number of downloads
1	Shooter	Hyper Casual
2	RPG	Match-3
3	Social Casino	Shooter

Source: Datamagic

80.47%

of users use Android smartphones and tablets, and 18.25% use iOS

106.22 GB

people in Turkey use this amount of mobile traffic in average yearly, while the Internet speed is 36.22 Mbit/s

8.5%

the percentage of average consumer spending per capita for recreation and culture made up by mobile games in Turkey

$0.09

is the average user acquisition cost for a mobile game

Turkish Culture

Language: Turkish.

National symbols: The evil eye, Turkish coffee, Turkish delight, Marash ice cream.

Other important cultural elements: flag (the crescent moon and star), Ataturk, Van Cat, Anatolian shepherd, tulips.

Main holidays:
New Year (January 1st), National Sovereignty and Children's Day (April 23rd) , Labor and Solidarity Day (May 1st), Commemoration of Ataturk, Youth and Sports Day (May 19th), Ramazan Bayrami Holiday (June 3rd–7th), Democracy and National Solidarity Day (July 15th), Kurban Bayrami Holiday (August 12th–15th), Victory Day (August 30th), Republic Day (October 29th).

Turkish coffee: the Turkish equivalent of the color brown (kahverengi) literally means "the color of coffee" in Turkish	Femininity	Sadness, death, mourning	Purity, marriage, innocence, cleanliness; secondary color of the flag	Masculinity	Nature, good	Urgency, blood, war, anger, but also the color of love; primary color of the national flag

Objectionable or forbidden themes: betting games are forbidden in Turkey. LGBT-related content isn't illegal per-se, but it might upset some players as it's still considered a taboo by the majority. Damaging the flag is also illegal, so showing something like that in a game might have consequences.

Top brands on mobile market in Turkey

Culturalization Case
Case: Cultural adaptation.

Situation: Since the game is based on a well-known American cartoon, it contains cultural nuances and references that might not make sense to a Turkish audience.

Solution: Find replacements for those instances. For example, "there's a Motel 6 on every corner in Virginia" was replaced with "there's a kebab stand on every corner in Europe."

4.24. Saudi Arabia

Market size+

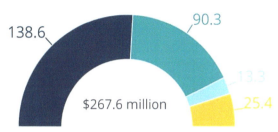

138.6
90.3
13.3
25.4

$267.6 million

in billions of US dollars

● Mobile games ● Downloaded games ● Online games

● Social games

Players' spending

Average spending for recreation and culture

$1058

Average spending for mobile games

$37

87%

use bank cards

6%

of women and 3% of men play every day for more than 5 hours

15%

of players are going to ?nish the game, and for 26% process is more important than result

43.65%

very low English fluency according to the EF EPI index

40%

of female players and 41% of male players are single

Population of Saudi Arabia

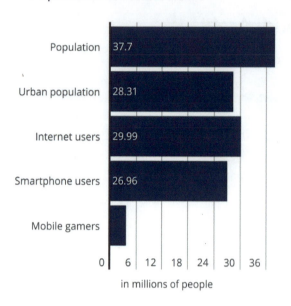

	in millions of people
Population	37.7
Urban population	28.31
Internet users	29.99
Smartphone users	26.96
Mobile gamers	

Number of gamers in Saudi Arabia

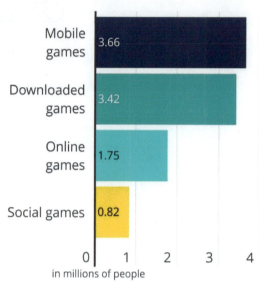

	in millions of people
Mobile games	3.66
Downloaded games	3.42
Online games	1.75
Social games	0.82

FACTS ABOUT GAMERS

Age and gender distribution

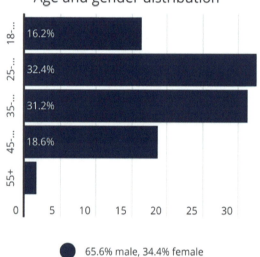

Age	
18-...	16.2%
25-...	32.4%
35-...	31.2%
45-...	18.6%
55+	

● 65.6% male, 34.4% female

Popular mobile game genres

№	By revenue	By number of downloads
1	Battle Royale	Battle Royale
2	Strategy	Match-3
3	Card games	Sport

Source: Datamagic

60%

of players use Android smartphones and tablets, and 30.19% of players use iOS

156.38 GB

of mobile traffic is used in Saudi Arabia by a person in average yearly, while the Internet speed is 37.53 Mbit/s

3.38%

the percentage of average consumer spending per capita for recreation and culture made up by mobile games in Saudi Arabia

$0.18

is the average user acquisition cost for a mobile game

4.25. Iran

Market size

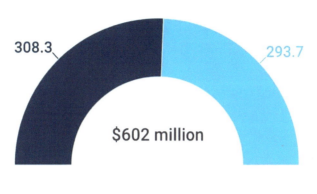

308.3

293.7

$602 million

● Mobile games ● PC & console games

Players' spending

Average spending for recreation and culture

$111

Average spending for mobile games

$13.12

26%
use e-wallets to pay

47%

of gamers play every day

19 years old

age of an average gamer

36.4%

very low English fluency according to the EF EPI index

78%

of gamers are single, 15% are married with children, 6% are married without children

Population of Iran

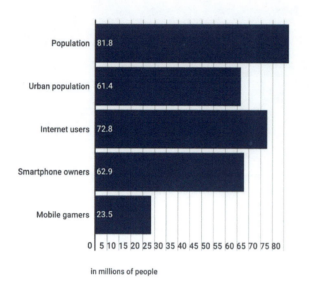

in millions of people

Number of gamers in Iran

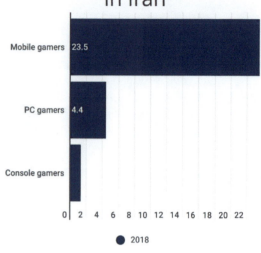

● 2018

in millions of people

FACTS ABOUT GAMERS

Age and gender distribution

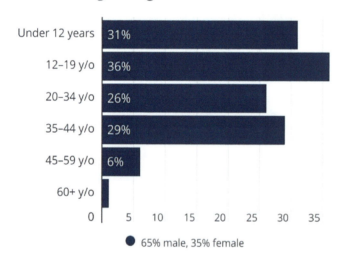

● 65% male, 35% female

Popular mobile game genres

1   Puzzle
2   Platformer/Runner
3   Racing/Driving
4   Sports
5   Arcade

87.31%

of players use Android smartphones and tablets, and 11.76% of players use iOS

163.28 GB

people in Iran use this amount of mobile traffic in average yearly, while the Internet speed is 28.39 Mbit/s

11.82%

the percentage of average consumer spending per capita for recreation and culture made up by mobile games in Iran

$0.23

is the average user acquisition cost for a mobile game

4.26. United Arab Emirates (UAE)

Market Size

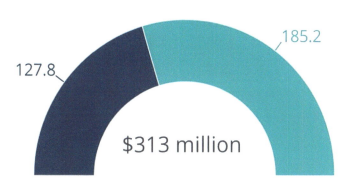

127.8

185.2

$313 million

● Mobile games   ● PC and console games

Players' spending

Average spending for recreation and culture

$1303

Average spending for mobile games

$47.33

60%
use cards to pay

66%
of players play every day

42%
have 5 game sessions or more

20–40 minutes
average daily time for mobile gaming

56.72%
average English fluency according to the EF EPI index

Population of UAE

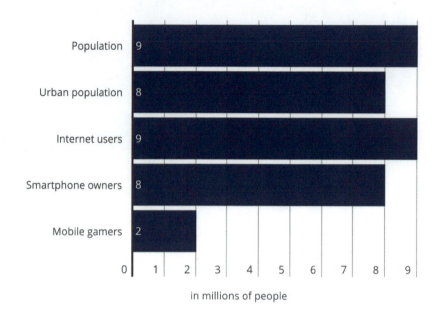

Population	9
Urban population	8
Internet users	9
Smartphone owners	8
Mobile gamers	2

in millions of people

FACTS ABOUT MOBILE GAMERS

Where do they play?

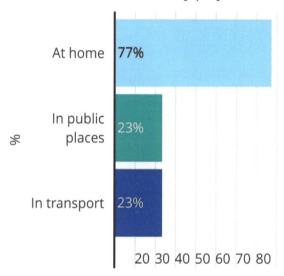

- At home 77%
- In public places 23%
- In transport 23%

%

20 30 40 50 60 70 80

67.14%

of users prefer Android, 21.15%—iOS

89.64 GB

people in UAE use this amount of mobile traffic in average yearly, while the Internet speed is 58.82 Mbit/s

$10.23

price of 1 GB of mobile Internet

$0.26

is the average user acquisition cost for a mobile game

Popular mobile game genres

№	By revenue	By number of downloads
1	Battle Royale	Battle Royale
2	Strategy	Match-3
3	RPG	Sport

4.27. Republic of South Africa (RSA)

Market size

174.9

41.1

$216 million

● Mobile games ● PC and console games

Players' spending

Average spending for recreation and culture

$167

Average spending for mobile games

$4.13

68%

use cards to pay

47%

of gamers work full-time, and 13% are unemployed and looking for a job

14%

of employees in RSA gamedev are female

66.52%

high English fluency according to the EF EPI index

Population of RSA

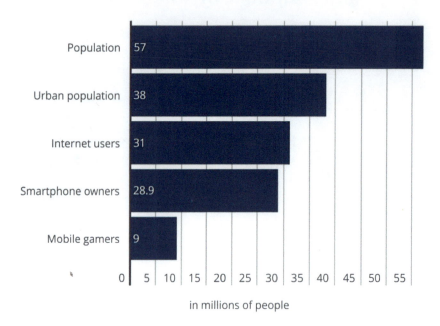

	in millions of people
Population	57
Urban population	38
Internet users	31
Smartphone owners	28.9
Mobile gamers	9

in millions of people

FACTS ABOUT MOBILE GAMERS

Age and gender distribution

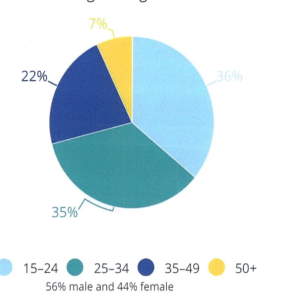

- 7%
- 22%
- 36%
- 35%

● 15–24 ● 25–34 ● 35–49 ● 50+

56% male and 44% female

Popular mobile game genres

№	By revenue	By number of downloads
1	Match-3	Shooter
2	Strategy	Puzzle
3	Farm	RPG

78.73%

of users prefer Android, 13.97% prefer iOS

11.4 GB

people in South Africa use this amount of mobile traffic in average yearly, while the Internet speed is 29.95 Mbit/s

$7.19

price of 1 GB of mobile Internet

$0.50

is the average user acquisition cost for a mobile game

114

4.28. Nigeria

Market size

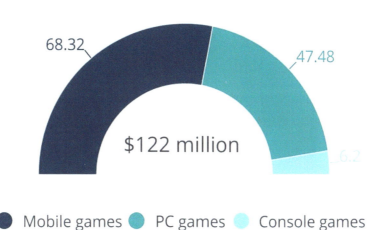

68.32

47.48

6.2

$122 million

● Mobile games ● PC games ● Console games

Players' spending

Average spending for recreation and culture

$24

$3

Average spending for mobile games

40%

use bank cards

49.5%

of gamers bought games or mobile apps at least once; 42.6% of users make ingame payments

97.11%

of gamers use Google for Internet searching

29 million

mobile transactions had been made in 2017

81%

persentage of mobile traffic

Population of Nigeria

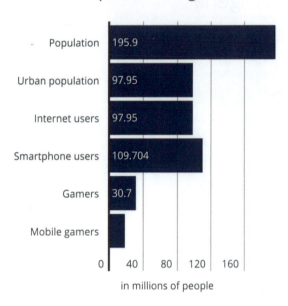

	in millions of people
Population	195.9
Urban population	97.95
Internet users	97.95
Smartphone users	109.704
Gamers	30.7
Mobile gamers	

Number of gamers in Nigeria

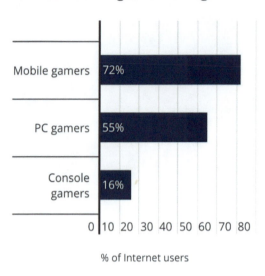

	% of Internet users
Mobile gamers	72%
PC gamers	55%
Console gamers	16%

FACTS ABOUT GAMERS

Age and gender distribution

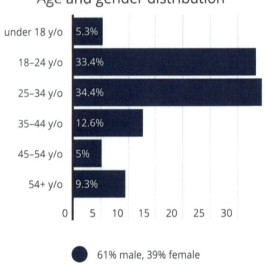

under 18 y/o	5.3%
18–24 y/o	33.4%
25–34 y/o	34.4%
35–44 y/o	12.6%
45–54 y/o	5%
54+ y/o	9.3%

● 61% male, 39% female

Popular mobile game genres

№	By revenue	By number of downloads
1	Match-3	Match-3
2	Shooter	Sport
3	Adventures	Action: Arcade

Source: Datamagic

72.72%

of users use Android, 3.71% use iOS

2.7 GB

of mobile traffic is used in Nigeria by a person in average yearly, while the Internet speed is 14 Mbit/s

16.56%

the percentage of average consumer spending per capita for recreation and culture made up by mobile games in Nigeria

$0.17

is the average user acquisition cost for a mobile game

5. Localization

5.1. Game Development Plan

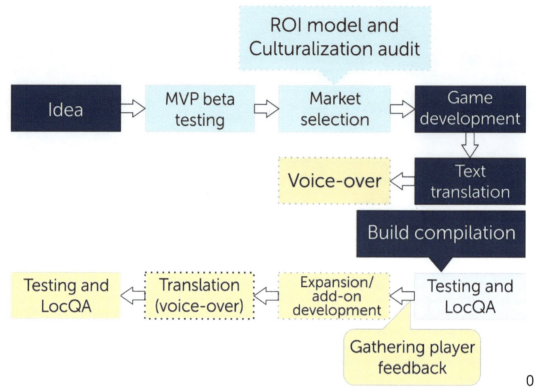

Dark blue: phases that are usually present.
Light blue: mandatory phases that are frequently forgotten.
Light yellow: extra phases.
Dotted line: whether the phase is present depends on the type of game.

5.2. What Developers Need to Know about Localization

Localizing a game involves translating its text in light of linguistic and cultural features with subsequent localization or linguistic testing.

5.2.1. The Six Commandments of Localization Prep[44]

When developing a game that will subsequently be localized, you need to[45]:
1. Separate internal resources (menus, character dialogs, multimedia content, etc., including numbers, punctuation, currency symbols, etc.) from the code and provide for them to be sorted by locale.
2. Store content for localization in convenient formats (PO, XLIFF).

---

[44] You can learn more about software localization and internationalization in the recommendations from Google and Apple.
[45] A Couple of Words about Software Internationalization

3. Use Unicode[46].

4. Provide for potential text length increases[47] during localization (by 30–200% depending on the number of words and language pair) for interface elements.

5. Make sure you will be able to move interface elements in various language versions and have a flexible variable order due to differences in syntax and orthography from language to language.

6. Avoid unnecessary optimization (for example, all the numbers the player doesn't see need to be separated from the code—their appearance will depend on the player's chosen font and language and could be very different from the numbers baked into the game's code and displayed by the system font).

5.2.2. Choosing a Font and Font Use in Games

If you need to use your own font for your game, use the[48] Unicode Character Database and International Components for Unicode[49] while developing it and store the font itself in TrueType (TTF) format—this format is supported by most systems, including Android and iOS.

5.2.2.1. Choosing a Font

When choosing a font, make sure it supports the writing systems of your chosen localization languages, e.g.:

1. The Latin alphabet (including the expanded alphabet) for Western European and some other languages
2. The Cyrillic alphabet (Russian, Serbian, etc.)
3. Languages with RTL writing such as Hebrew and Arabic
4. Character-based writing systems such as Chinese and Japanese
5. The writing systems of Southeast Asia, India, etc.

All in all, we suggest using different fonts for Western European countries, Middle Eastern countries, and Asian and Southeastern Asian countries.

There are many different paid and free resources for choosing fonts that allow you to sort them by supported languages. A partial list can be found below:

---

[46]The Unicode Standard
[47]Text translation design
[48]Unicode Character Database
[49]ICU—International Components for Unicode

Portal name	Free fonts and sorting by language	Note
Google Fonts	yes	
Fonts.com	yes	
MyFonts	yes	
Adobe Fonts	yes	no fonts that support Japanese, Chinese, and a few other languages
Webtype	no	

5.2.2.2. Font Use in Games

Recommendations on using fonts in games (appropriate for European languages)[50]:

- Serif fonts are suitable for applications or in-game texts with a large number of words (such as books). Sans-serif fonts are suitable for interfaces.
- Modern fonts (such as, for example, San Francisco in iOS) have different typefaces that need to be used depending on the type of text (header) and font size.
- To choose a font size, you can use the golden ratio principle (1:1.618) as a multiplier for each step or a calculator[51].
- The minimum contrast coefficient for font sections is 4.5:1, while the recommended is 7:1. When choosing a font's contrast with the background, use this guide from W3[52] and Color Contrast Checker[53].
- Line spacing should be 120–145% of the size of the font. If it is less than that, the text will look squished and be hard to read.
- In order to ensure a smooth reading experience, each line should ideally contain 45-90 characters.
- Use large bold fonts for headers and gray medium 14-15 pt. fonts for subscripts (for mobile apps).

To see what a font will look like in an Android app, you can use Android Design Preview[54], and for online games you can use Web Font Specimen[55] or Typecast[56]. If you

---

[50] Typography in ten minutes
[51] Modular Scale
[52] W3C. Understanding WCAG 2.0
[53] WebAIM. Contrast Checker
[54] Google Code
[55] Web Font Specimen
[56] Typecast

are using multiple fonts in the same locale, you can check their visual compatibility using Discover.typography[57].

Even if you follow all of these recommendations and choose suitable fonts, you still need to test the game after importing the text. Unicode currently has a number of unresolved issues withdisplaying characters in character-based languages, languages that use the Arabic alphabet, and some other languages[58].

5.2.3. Choosing a Localization Contractor

Below you will find a table comparing different types of localization. What type of contractor and localization suits you best depends on a number of factors, such as whether or not you have a localization manager, your game development MO, how much you are willing to immerse yourself in the process, your budget, and many other things. For the majority of developers, hiring one person who would be responsible for managing localization within one or several companies should be enough.

Service Parameter / Localization model	Immersion in your product	Speed of access to resource	Resource scalability (scope of languages, output of work)	Resource reliability (dependability, consistency of service)	Workflow maturity (standardization quality control, tools proficiency, integrated localization engineering)	Management overhead savings (time and money)	Warranties (your contractual leverage)	Price
In-house translators	★★★	★★★	★☆☆	★★★	★★☆	★☆☆	★★★	★★☆
Freelancers	★★☆	★★☆	★★★	★☆☆	★★☆	★★☆	★★☆	★★☆
Crowdsourcing	★★★	★☆☆	★☆☆	★☆☆	★☆☆	★☆☆	★☆☆	★★★
Publicly available machine translation engine	☆☆☆	★★★	★★★	★★☆	☆☆☆	★★★	☆☆☆	★★★
Agency	★★☆	★★★	★★★	★★☆	★★★	★★★	★★★	★☆☆

A diagram of the localization process is shown below (based on Allcorrect's approach):

[57] Discover.typography
[58] Refer to the Problems with Unicode section

When working with localizers, a developer can be led by two main principles (besides common sense and meeting work and payment deadlines):

- Submit texts that are either finished or as close to finished as possible.
- Localize assignments in chunks that are as big as possible.

Below we've tried to note the most important factors that need to be considered when planning a game's development. The later the developer plans the steps in this checklist[59], the more it might cost them in the long-run.

	Yes/No	Notes
Project Management		
Have the languages for localization been selected?		
Are there deadlines on the localization?		
Is there an agreed-upon localization budget?		
Who will manage the localization process within the company?		
Who will translate the game? (freelancers, in-house translators, a company, multiple companies)		
Who will handle QA for translation, voice-over, and testing within the company?		
Will the text change after the localization launches?		

---

[59]This checklist is based on Localization Overview Checklist from The Game Localization Handbook and Allcorrect's project specifications for clients and translators.

Who will submit localized versions of the game for an age rating to be assigned to them?		
On which platforms will the game be released?		
What are the project's goals, success metrics, and target audience?		
Integration		
The game's text supports Unicode (including RTL languages)		
Linguistic locales can be easily integrated into the game		
Localized keyboard support		
Buttons can be expanded in the game's interface		
Your localizer can work with the format of your texts for localization		
Support for various kinds of dates and exchange rates		
Localization version management system		
Is there a tested process for loading text into and out of the game?		
Will subtitles need to be added to the game?		
Who will match the text to the voice-over?		
Is there a tested process for loading audio files for voice-over into and out of the game?		
Devices required for testing		
Is there a test plan?		
Whose bug-tracking system will you use?		
Specific translation requirements		
Stylistic preferences for the translation (formal, informal)		
String length limitations		
Are abbreviations with periods acceptable?		

For example, "approximately" as "approx."		
Formal or informal mode of address to the player (only applicable for certain languages)		
Capitalization requirements (will terms be capitalized or not?)		
Use of profane language		
References to sex, violence, etc.		

Most localization companies (and translators) translate from English into all other languages. If your source language is something other than English, you'll want to set time aside not just to have it translated into English, but also to have it proofread.

Three key factors in the localization process are time frames, quality, and cost. Let's take a quick look at each of them.

5.2.3.1. Time frames

The time frames of a localization can depend on which phases of the localization process have been planned, as well as the quality of that planning.

Main limitations during translation:
1. A translator can provide a high-quality translation of about 1,700–2,000 words a day[60].
2. An editor can edit up to 3,000–4,000 words a day.
3. Translators' and editors' time zones.

Keep in mind that modern computer-assisted translation software makes it possible to begin translating and editing into all languages virtually simultaneously.

Main limitations during testing:
1. Testers' time zones
2. Having a test plan
3. Having a cheat system
4. Testers spend time not only playing the game, but also making corrections and filling in bug reports.
5. In order to keep testers focused, the amount of time dedicated purely to testing (without factoring in the time it takes to make corrections and draw up reports) should not exceed five hours a day.

---

[60] Translation services - Requirements for translation services.

Main limitations during voice-over:

1. A recording room can only record one actor at a time.

2. A voice-over actor cannot work more than 4-5 hours a day. Longer sessions can have an adverse effect on their health and lead to vocal cord injuries. This is connected to the unique nature of video game voice-over, including the need to read out phrases outside of context and suddenly shift between high and low vocal pitches.

3. Restrictions on the length of voice-over segments need to be specified in advance. The same applies to any technical requirements for the recording, including frequency, volume, effects, compression, file format, etc.

4. In addition to recording, you need to set time aside for mixing, cutting audio tracks, and adding effects.

You also need to give the director a chance to familiarize themselves with the game, its characters, the history of the world, the script, and other context so they can get the right intonation and appropriate emotion from the actors.

Any evaluation, including that of localization quality, must:
1. Be reproducible (i.e. be confirmed by other evaluators).
2. Be repeatable (the same person examines the text after a certain amount of time and has basically the same evaluation).
3. Be as impartial and objective as possible.
4. Satisfy the objectives that have been set (when evaluating someone's performance).

When evaluating the quality of a translation, we recommend using the model developed by Logrus IT[61]. This model is based on the principle of an empirical evaluation of the text where the focus is set on the overall meaning and style of the final translation, and not just a tally of mistakes. This approach makes it possible to quickly determine whether a text is ready to be published and read by the end consumer or needs to be revised and touched up. In addition, this model meets the evaluation parameters described above.

Translation quality can be determined indirectly using subsequent testing (standards of quality, acceptable number of bugs, errors, etc.), and sometimes via player feedback. We already have a tool that allows us to find and extract player comments and feedback related to localization quality, then sort them by language and divide them into positive and negative. In addition, we can also identify new markets where there is a demand for translation.

Testing quality can be evaluated in three steps:
1. Cross-checking the game (have all the bugs been found?)
2. Checking bug reports to ensure the client's requirements have been met
3. Totaling up error indicators (the number of missed bugs and errors when drawing up bug reports)

Voice-over quality can be measured objectively based on the following parameters:
1. Sound quality, volume, and presence of extraneous noise
2. Adherence to time requirements regarding the length of voice-over segments; whether or not the lip sync or waveform matches the audio
3. The appropriateness of the voice actors' intonations
4. Whether phrases and subtitles match
5. Whether the in-game context matches the recording

---

[61] Reliably Measuring Something That Isn't Completely Objective: The Quality Triangle Approach to Translation Quality Assurance. Leonid Glazychev. Logrus IT, USA

5.2.3.3. Localization Cost

Translation cost is calculated based on the number of words to be translated and can include discounts for large text volumes and repetitions as well as additional charges for urgency and small text volumes. The cost of translation typically ranges from USD 0.10 to USD 0.20 per word depending on the language pair.

The cost of testing is based on working hours and depends on the number of testers (languages) and platforms required.

The cost of voice-over is also based on working hours, as well as the number of characters being voiced and the actors required for this. The final cost can also be affected by:
1. Requirements for the studio's recording equipment
2. Hiring famous voice actors
3. Limitations on phrase length and lip sync

Below you can find an outline of a localization project, as well as a budget quote for each kind of work.

The example involves a hypothetical project for an online mobile game with 40,000 words and translation into three languages (including 5,000 words of voice-over), as well as 50 hours of localization testing.

	Translation	USD 14 800,00
	Voiceover	USD 10 800,00
	Localization testing (LQA)	USD 5 900,00
	Total	USD 31 500,00

Description	Language pair	Volume	UoM	Rate	Total
Translation	English - French	40 000	Word	0.15	6000,00
Translation	English - German	40 000	Word	0.15	6000,00
Translation	English - Russian	40 000	Word	0.07	2800,00
Voiceover	English - Russian	9	Hour	400,000	3600,00
Voiceover	English - German	9	Hour	400,000	3600,00
Voiceover	English - French	9	Hour	400,000	3600,00
Localization testing (LQA)	English - Russian	50	Hour	18,000	900,00
Localization testing (LQA)	English - French	50	Hour	50,000	2500,00
Localization testing (LQA)	English - German	50	Hour	50,000	2500,00

	Task name	July 28	Aug 4	Aug 11	Aug 18	Aug 25	Sep 1	Sep 8	Sep 15	Sep 22
1	Project pre-production									
2	Pre-translation analysis: analysis of the technical features of the file, analysis of ID and placeholder values, analysis of the stylistic features of the game, evaluation of the literary aspects of the text, cultural analysis (determining whether or not the text is appropriate for the audience and identifying any aspects of the text that could be received negatively by players of various cultures)									
3	Coordination of the features of work on the project, confirming the localization specification									
4	Configuration of CAT tools to meet the needs of the project									
5	Assembling the team									
6	Selecting 10% of the text as a sample of translation									
7										
8	Translation									
9	Batch 1									
10	Pre-production									
11	Translation									
12	English - Russian									
13	English - French									
14	English - German									
15	Editing/Review									
16	English - Russain									
17	English - French									
18	English - German									
19	Cross-checking									
20	VO (All languages)									
21	Proofreading of VO (All languages)									
22	LQA (All languages)									
23	Bug validation (All languages)									
24										
25										

Appendix and Data Tables

1. Sizes of Mobile Game Markets by Language[62]

#	Language[63]	Countries	Population	Mobile Gamers	Revenue
1	Simplified Chinese	China	1,435,000,000	601,000,000	USD 19,400,000,000
2	English	Australia, Canada, India, Ireland, Kenya, New Zealand, Nigeria, Philippines, Singapore, South Africa, United Kingdom, United States	874,267,700	254,419,010	USD 23,162,598,700
3	Japanese	Japan	127,200,000	46,880,000	USD 11,100,000,000
4	Spanish (Mex)	Argentina, Chile, Colombia, Ecuador, Mexico, Peru, United States, Uruguay, Venezuela	372,518,000	106,215,550	USD 3,225,700,000
5	Korean	South Korea	51,200,000	32,100,000	USD 3,200,000,000
6	German	Austria, German, Switzerland	98,079,500	21,304,950	USD 1,865,205,500
7	French	Belgium, Canada, France, Switzerland	81,926,700	21,959,750	USD 1,270,482,300
8	Hindi	India	1,170,504,800	187,637,500	USD 883,000,000

[62]Listed in descending order by mobile games market size. Data on populations, number of games, and mobile games market taken from Statista. Mobile Games Outlook, Newzoo and others for 2018
[63]Data on native speakers for 2018 is taken from several sources: www.ethnologue.com, www.internetworldstats.com, www.en.wikipedia.org, www.infoplease.com, and www.worldatlas.com. The only languages considered were the ones for which the percentage share of the respective native speakers amounted to at least 10% of the total population of the country. If less than 100% of total population speak the selected languages, the data was adjusted to add up to 100%. No more than three languages were considered for each country. For countries with great language diversity, the language used for intertribal communications was assumed to be the primary language of the country (for example, English in Nigeria)

9	Russian	Russia	145,700,000	26,130,000	USD 715,900,000
10	Traditional Chinese	Hong Kong, Singapore, Taiwan	34,477,400	11,668,580	USD 713,785,400
11	Indonesian	Indonesia	267,700,000	60,000,000	USD 700,000,000
12	Portuguese (Bra)	Brazil	209,500,000	55,480,000	USD 580,000,000
13	Arabic	Egypt, Saudi Arabia, United Arab Emirates	142,500,000	27,320,000	USD 542,100,000
14	Italian	Italy	60,600,000	13,910,000	USD 525,100,000
15	Turkish	Turkey	82,300,000	11,020,000	USD 400,000,000
16	Spanish	Spain	46,700,000	9,150,000	USD 335,120,000
17	Vietnamese	Vietnam	96,500,000	37,280,000	USD 322,000,000
18	Persian	Iran	81,800,000	23,500,000	USD 308,300,000
19	Dutch	Belgium, Netherlands	24,000,000	5,854,000	USD 217,480,000
20	Polish	Poland	38,100,000	4,700,000	USD 128,400,000
21	Swedish	Sweden	10,000,000	2,290,000	USD 115,600,000
22	Thai	Thailand	69,400,000	3,250,000	USD 86,100,000
23	Urdu	Pakistan	200,800,000	14,760,000	USD 85,500,000
24	Bokmål	Norway	5,400,000	1,230,000	USD 79,400,000
25	Danish	Denmark	5,800,000	750,000	USD 54,700,000
26	Malay	Malaysia	32,000,000	4,000,000	USD 54,300,000

27	Hebrew	Israel	8,500,000	1,020,000	USD 49,800,000
28	Finnish	Finland	5,500,000	960,000	USD 44,700,000
29	Tagalog	Philippines	58,575,000	2,073,500	USD 37,125,000
30	Czech	Czech Republic	10,600,000	1,510,000	USD 34,300,000
31	Singhalese	Sri Lanka	16,800,000	2,936,000	USD 31,360,000
32	Portuguese	Portugal	10,300,000	1,140,000	USD 28,600,000
33	Romanian	Romania	19,600,000	1,700,000	USD 23,200,000
34	Hungarian	Hungary	9,700,000	1,270,000	USD 17,500,000
35	Swahili	Kenya	25,500,000	2,255,000	USD 13,800,000
36	Zulu	South Africa	13,661,200	2,370,480	USD 9,781,800
37	Tamil	Sri Lanka	4,200,000	734,000	USD 7,840,000
38	Afrikaans	South Africa	7,634,200	1,324,680	USD 5,466,300

2. Sizes of Game Markets

#	Country	Games market volume[64] (USD millions)	Mobile games market volume[65] (USD millions)	CPI[66], (USD)	EF EPI[67] (degree of English language proficiency)
1	China	37,945	19,400[68]	1.32	51.94 (low)
2	United States of America	30,411	13,000[69]	4.71	-
3	Japan	19,231	11,100	5.35	51.8 (low)
4	South Korea	5,647	3,200	3.66	56.27 (average)
5	UK	5,337	1552	4.25	-
6	Germany	4,057[70]	1780[71]	4.08	63.74 (very high)
7	France	3,131	595.3		55.49 (average)
8	Canada	2,303	377.4	5.12	-
9	Russia	1,669	715.9	2.17	52.96 (average)
10	Mexico	1,580	600		49.76 (low)

[64]Top 100 Countries/Markets by Game Revenues for 2018. Newzoo

[65]Data taken from Statista. Mobile Games Outlook, 2018, except for the data highlighted in blue, which comes from Newzoo, 2018 and a separate appendix. The data highlighted in yellow cannot be considered sufficiently reliable

[66]Data highlighted in green is taken from Mobile Gaming Apps Report 2019 User Acquisition Trends & Benchmarks, June 2018—May 2019. Liftoff. Everything else is either provided by Chartboost (March 2019 data takes into account user split for different mobile operating systems) or Statcounter (average statistics for 2018)

[67]The world's largest ranking of countries and regions by English skills, 2018. The average statistic for 2018 equals to 53.49

[68]USD 23 billion according to earlier Newzoo data as well as KrASIA data, and USD 15.83 bln according to Niko Partners data

[69]App Annie, 2018

[70] 3.435 bln euros—game sales + 0.96 bln euros (which equates to USD 5.2 bln dollars if using the mean 2018 exchange rate)—gaming hardware sales according to the German Games Industry Association data

[71]1.507 bln euros according to the German Games Industry Association data

11	Italy	1,570	525		55.77 (average)
12	Brazil	1,450	580	1.42	50.93 (low)
13	Taiwan	1,268	646.68		51.88 (low)
14	Spain	1,231	335		55.85 (average)
15	India	1,169	1000		57.13 (average)
16	Indonesia	1,130	700		51.58 (low)
17	Turkey	853	400		47.17 (very low)
18	Saudi Arabia	761	138.6		43.65 (very low)
19	Thailand	692	86.1		48.54 (very low)
20	Malaysia	654	54.3		59.32 (high)
21	Iran	602	308.3		48.29 (very low)
22	Vietnam	490	45.5		53.12 (average)
23	Philippines	478	67.5		61.84 (high)
24	Hong Kong	381	41.9		56.38 (average)
25	Singapore	330	41.8		68.63 (very high)
26	United Arab Emirates	313	127.8		47.27 (very low)
27	South Africa	216[72]	41.1		66.52 (high)
28	Nigeria	122	68.32[73]		56.72 (average)

[72] Newzoo, 2018
[73] Approximated data—calculated by multiplying games market sales by smartphone penetration

3. Demographic Data[74]

#	Country	Population[75] (millions)	Median age[76]	Urban population[77] (%)	Number of players[78] (millions)	Number of mobile gamers (millions)
1	China	1,435	38.70	59	619.5	601[79]
2	India	1,325.6	28.20	34	250[80]	212.5
3	United States of America	327.1	38.30	82	178.7[81]	160.93
4	Indonesia	267.7	29.30	55		117.76
5	Philippines	106.7	25.20	47		63.64
6	Japan	127.2	48.20	92	67.6	58.6[82]
7	Brazil	209.5	33.50	87	75.7	55.48
8	Thailand	69.4	38.10	50		46.6
9	Vietnam	95.5	32.60	36		37.28
10	Mexico	126.2	29.30	80	55.8	34.38
11	South Korea	51.2	43.40	81	28.9	27[83]
12	Russia	145.7	39.60	74	62.5	26.1

[74]Markets are listed in descending order by number of mobile gamers
[75]Data on population and number of mobile gamers: Statista. Mobile Games Outlook, 2018.
[76]Median age of population. Digital 2019. Data on corresponding countries, 2018
[77] United Nations Population Division. World Urbanization Prospects: 2018 Revision
[78]2018 data taken from Newzoo Infographics
[79]According to KrASIA data, Additional data: 721.1 mln according to Newzoo data, 626 mln according to iResearch data, 598 mln (95% of all gamers) according to Niko Partners data, and 424.06 mln according to Statista data
[80] The evolving landscape of sports gaming in India, KPMG, 2018 data
[81] 211.2 mln—90% of these people play mobile games according to EEDAR data, and 203 mln according Mediakix data
[82]70 mln according to Newzoo data
[83]32.1 mln according to Newzoo data

13	Iran	81.8	30.80	75		23.5
14	Germany	83.1	46.60	77	34[84]	18.6[85]
15	Nigeria	195.9	18.10	50	30,7	17
16	UK	67.1	40.80	83	37.3	17
17	France	65	42.00	80	32.8	16.51
18	Italy	60.6	47.90	70	26.2	13.91
19	Canada	37.1	41.40	81	21.2[86]	12.6
20	Turkey	82.3	31.40	75	30	11.02
21	South Africa	57.8	27.30	66		9.96
22	Taiwan	23.58[87]	42.2	77.5[88]	14.5	9.5[89]
23	Spain	46.7	45.50	80	24.6	9.15
24	Malaysia	31.5	29.90	76	17,7	4
25	Saudi Arabia	33.7	31.90	84		3.66
26	United Arab Emirates	9.6	30.30	87		2.7
27	Hong Kong	7.4	44.80	100		1.65
28	Singapore	5.8	34.90	100		0.86

---

[84] 34 mln according to the German Games Industry Association data

[85] 18.6 mln play games on their smartphones and another 10.9 mln, on their tablets according to the German Games Industry Association data

[86] Over 23 mln according to ESAC data

[87] Trading Economics, 2018

[88] Worldometers, 2018

[89] Approximated statistic, taken from Newzoo, 2018

4. Structure of Player Spendings[90]

#	Country	Average yearly spending[91] on recreation, sports, and culture (USD)	Annual gamer ARPU[92] (USD)	Annual mobile gamer ARPU (USD)	Percentage share of annual spending on mobile games among total spending on recreation (%)
1	Vietnam	14		13	
2	India	11	5	7	
3	Thailand	46		26	
4	Philippines	42		18	
5	China	398	61	27	6.76%
6	Japan	1,560	284	159	10.16%
7	Indonesia	122		15	12.17%
8	Iran	111		13	
9	Brazil	61	20	6	9.78%
10	South Korea	1,138		100	8.76%
11	Mexico	355	29	20	5.76%
12	Nigeria	24		1	
13	Russia	492	27	27	5.58%

---

[90]Listed in descending order by percentage share of spendings on mobile games among total spendings on recreation. Majority of data taken from: Statista. Mobile Games Outlook, 2018. Percentage share of spendings on mobile games was calculated using data from reliable sources only

[91]Using the following UN Classification: Classification of Individual Consumption According to Purpose (COICOP), 2018

[92]Data taken from Newzoo's Top 100 Countries/Markets by Game Revenues for 2018 and other sources

14	United Arab Emirates	1,303		47	
15	Saudi Arabia	1,058		38	
16	UK	2,472	119	74	3.01%
17	Turkey	427		12	2.74%
18	Malaysia	511		14	
19	Spain	1,273	83	33	2.57%
20	South Africa	167		4	
21	Italy	1,382	77	30	2.17%
22	United States of America	3,497	170	75	2.15%
23	France	1,697	95	36	2.12%
24	Singapore	2,296		49	
25	Germany	2,108	106	32	1.51%
26	Canada	2,058	109	30	1.46%
27	Hong Kong	2008			
28	Taiwan		87	68	

5. Internet Access[93]

#	Country	Internet penetration[94] (%)	Smartphone penetration (%)	Average yearly spending on communications[95] (USD)	Average cost[96] of 1 GB of data (USD)	Average internet speed[97] (Mbps)	Annual mobile internet traffic volume[98] (GB)
1	Malaysia	80	77	580	1.18	21.26	491.53
2	Italy	92	85	461	1.73	32.93	266.47
3	Hong Kong	89	82	968	4	32.26	242.00
4	Russia	64	76	219	0.91	20.12	240.66
5	France	92	74	528	2.99	45.83	176.59
6	Iran	89	77	209	1.28	28.39	163.28
7	Saudi Arabia	89	80	880	5.62	37.53	156.58
8	India	41	40	39	0.26	11.02	150.00
9	Spain	93	86	451	3.79	33.7	119.00
10	Brazil	70	66	414	3.5	21.39	118.29
11	Singapore	84	79	425	3.67	53.47	115.80
12	Turkey	72	68	239	2.25	36.22	106.22
13	Japan	94	78	855	8.34	30.85	102.52

---

[93]Listed in descending order by affordability of mobile internet
[94]Data on internet and smartphone penetration taken from DataReportal reports for corresponding countries, 2018
[95]Using the following UN Classification: Classification of Individual Consumption According to Purpose (COICOP), 2018. Qualitative data taken from Statista
[96]Worldwide mobile data pricing: The cost of 1GB of mobile data in 230 countries, October 23—November 28, 2018
[97]Speedtest Global Index, May 2019
[98]Limited to users who only spend on mobile internet

14	Germany	96	78	660	6.96	31.9	94.83
15	Indonesia	56	53	112	1.21	11.7	92.56
16	United Arab Emirates	99	91	917	10.23	58.82	89.64
17	UK	95	80	492	6.66	30.93	73.87
18	United States of America	95	82	883	12.37	35	71.38
19	Thailand	82	79	184	2.78	19.23	66.19
20	Canada	91	74	681	12.02	63.81	56.66
21	Vietnam	66	64	63	1.31	25.3	48.09
22	South Korea	95	90	417	15.12	76.74	27.58
23	Mexico	67	62	188	7.38	23.78	25.47
24	Philippines	71	67	66	3.16	15.1	20.89
25	South Africa	54	50	82	7.19	29.95	11.40
26	China	57	54	110	9.89	33.72	11.12
27	Nigeria	50	46	6	2.22	14	2.70
28	Taiwan	88	82		9.49	43.49	

6. Payment Statistics by Country[99]

#	Country	Bank account ownership percentage share[100] (%)	Most popular payment systems for online purchases	Refunds[101] (%)	Payment frauds[102] (%)	Data year[103]
1	India	79.9	65.4% cards[104]		4-5	2017
2	Brazil	70	59% cards	3.55		2017
3	Mexico	37	45% cards	2.82		2016
4	Russia	87.9[105]	88.9%[106] cards	0.82	0.75	2018
5	United States of America	93	71.5% cards	0.47		2017
6	China	80.2	54% digital wallets	0.1	0.2	2017
7	UK	96.4	78% cards	0.08	6.06	2018
8	Germany	99.1	26% digital wallets	0.08	0.49	2018
9	France	94	53.9% cards	0.06	2.88	2018
10	Spain	93.8	43.2% cards	0.06	1.29	2018

[99]Table includes data on indicators available online
[100]J.P. Morgan 2019 Payments Trends, 2017 and 2018 data
[101]Refunds are partially caused by payment frauds. On average, the higher the share of refunds, the greater the number of payment frauds in the country. Countries are listed in descending order by percentage share of refunds
[102]Data on payment frauds in Europe: Fico.Total Threat Levels, 2018
[103]Data on refunds and payment frauds highlighted in yellow is taken from Top 12 Countries Exposed to Chargeback Fraud for 2016 and from J.P. Morgan 2019 Payments Trends–Global Insights Report for the remaining years. Data on percentage shares of refunds and payment frauds may vary greatly from year to year
[104]Here and onwards highlighted in blue—Going Global: Payment Insights to Achieve Growth at Scale, Mastercard. 2017 data
[105]Russian payment card market: overview, 2016 data
[106]Online Payments in Russia: 2018 Mediascope report, 2018 data

11	Italy	93.8	33.8% cards	0.06	0.5	2018
12	Japan	92.8	65% cards		0.1	2018
13	Malaysia	85	46% wired transfers		0.02	2018
14	Iran[107]	94	26% digital wallets			2017
15	Vietnam[108]	31	34% cards			2017
16	Turkey	69	64% cards			2017
17	Singapore	98	79% cards			2017
18	Indonesia	48	34% cards			2017
19	Hong Kong	95.3	49% cards			2017
20	Thailand	81	30% cards			2017
21	Saudi Arabia	72[109]	87%[110] cards			2017
22	Nigeria[111]	40	5.6% digital wallets			2017
23	United Arab Emirates	88[112]	60% cards[113]			2017
24	Canada	99.8	62% cards			2017
25	South Korea[114]	95	66% cards			2017

[107] Digital 2019 Iran
[108] We Are Social Vietnam 2019 | Vietnam digital landscape 2019 report, 2018 and 2019 data
[109] Digital 2019 Saudi Arabia
[110] ICT Report. E-Commerce in Saudi Arabia, 2017 data
[111] Digital 2019 Nigeria
[112] Digital 2019 United Arab Emirates
[113] Going Global: Payment Insights to Achieve Growth at Scale, 2016 data
[114] Digital 2019 South Korea

26	Philippines[115]	34	54% cards			2017
27	Taiwan		75.7% cards[116]			2017
28	South Africa[117]	69	68% cards			2017

[115] Digital 2019 Philippines
[116] Taiwan Country Commercial Guide. Taiwan - ECommerce
[117] Digital 2019 South Africa

Intellectual Property

All infographics in the guide were made using Infogram. Brands and trademarks mentioned, including, but not limited to Samsung, Sony, Nintendo, Microsoft and others belong to their respective owners. The illustrations for the culturalization slides were taken from public sources (Pinterest, etc.) online.

Authors

Denis Khamin (Chapters 1-4, 5.1, 5.2, 5.2.3, appendix, source analysis)

Valentine Pronin (Chapters 5.2.3.1-5.2.3.3)

Demid Tishin (table in Chapter 5.2.3)

Marina Lekhina, Dmitrii Antonov, Tatyana Veryasova (collecting data culture-specific traits in each country for Chapter 4 infographics)

Artur Karniev (compiling infographics)

Yulia Poskonina (layout and composition)

Alexandra Siluyanova (project management)

English translators: Nathan Klausner, Jared Firth, Krystal Tarasova, Natalia Glinskaya, Alexey Osokin, Anton Stepanov.

The authors would like to express their thanks for consulting, suggestions, and comments to Demid Tishin, Darya Tvorilova, Lilia Efremenko, Tatyana Veryasova, Igor Sheynikov, Roman Zhin, Marina Turkina, Marina Ilyinykh, Konstantin Dranch, André Espinha, Suratina Hapsari, Danh Chieu Phu Hyunh, Nouri Adam, Peerapon Jamsirirojrat, Ashutosh Mitra, Smallwood Stuart, Gonzalez Manuel Gordillo, Mariana Ruiz, Ali Yucel.

Sources

www.ingramcontent.com/pod-product-compliance
Lightning Source LLC
Chambersburg PA
CBHW041426050326

40689CB00003B/680